create with
CORK FABRIC

Sew 17 Upscale Projects

Bags, Accessories & Home Decor

Jessica Sallie Kapitanski

stashBOOKS®

an imprint of C&T Publishing

Publisher: Amy Marson

Creative Director: Gailen Runge

Acquisitions Editor: Roxane Cerda

Managing Editor: Liz Aneloski

Editor: Beth Baumgartel

Technical Editor: Helen Frost

Cover/Book Designer: April Mostek

Production Coordinator: Tim Manibusan

Production Editor: Jennifer Warren

Illustrator: Aliza Shalit

Photo Assistant: Rachel Holmes

Photography by Kelly Burgoyne of C&T Publishing, Inc.

Published by Stash Books, an imprint of C&T Publishing, Inc., P.O. Box 1456, Lafayette, CA 94549

Library of Congress Cataloging-in-Publication Data

Names: Kapitanski, Jessica Sallie, author.

Title: Create with cork fabric : sew 17 upscale projects; bags, accessories & home decor / Jessica Sallie Kapitanski.

Description: Lafayette, CA : C&T Publishing, Inc., [2019]

Identifiers: LCCN 2018058754 | ISBN 9781617458200 (soft cover)

Subjects: LCSH: Machine sewing. | Cork craft—Patterns.

Classification: LCC TT715 .K37 2019 | DDC 646.2/044--dc23

LC record available at https://lccn.loc.gov/2018058754

Printed in the USA

10 9 8 7 6 5 4 3 2

ACKNOWLEDGMENTS

To my best friend and husband, Mitch. Thank you for not only being involved but for also being interested in my endeavors and passions. Because of you, I got my business off the ground and created the career of my dreams. I love you and our life together!

An eternal thank-you to my parents for teaching me how to be creative, work hard, and follow my dreams. Without your support and confidence in my abilities, I would not have grown into the woman I am today. You both mean so much to me. I love you!

A special thank-you to my brother, Jacob. Despite our five-year age gap, we've always been great friends and supported each other. It's always a good time when you're around. Thank you for seeing the potential of my business and helping me grow! I love you, Jay!

To my in-laws, Val and Robert. You've always made me feel welcome and part of your family. Thank you for all your support and encouragement, which typically translates to heavy lifting and baby duty. You are always there for us, and I love you both.

To my Nancy's Notions family and all the teachers throughout my life—you know who you are! Thank you immensely for your words of wisdom and your confidence in me throughout the years.

Thank you to my editor, Beth Baumgartel, and the wonderful team at C&T Publishing. You all brought the best out of my vision for this book and made it truly beautiful. Thank you for your enthusiasm, attention to detail, and guidance.

A huge thank-you to the fabric companies and suppliers who generously donated the gorgeous fabric and threads for this book. Your quality materials brought this book to life!

Lastly, a sentimental thank-you to my loud and loving grandma. Without your love of sewing and crafting, this book would have never been possible. You've always inspired me. I miss your hugs and love you very much.

contents

SEW
APPY

introduction

My love of cork fabric began the moment I felt how soft and pliable it was. I had always thought of cork as stiff and brittle, but I soon found out how wrong I was. After sewing with cork fabric for the first time, I was hooked.

My first project with cork fabric involved making purse straps. The cork made the purse very comfortable to carry and gave it a professional touch. This first project quickly led to more. I progressed to using cork for accents as well as straps, and I've even made entire bags, home decor items, and jewelry out of cork. Cork's natural stability and texture makes it a go-to material in my fabric stash. There are numerous colors and textures to choose from, which makes cork a great fabric for all kinds of projects and for all seasons.

I've thoroughly tested and researched cork fabric so I can share the variety of benefits and sewing struggles you might encounter. I have broken needles and pushed sewing machines to their limits so you don't have to. I have learned the dos and don'ts so I can share them with you and so you'll enjoy sewing with cork fabric every time.

I wrote this book because I don't want you to be afraid of sewing with this unique material. Each of the projects in this book includes basic techniques for sewing with cork; it's my hope that as you work through the projects, your confidence will increase and you'll be inspired to pursue other projects that use cork fabric.

Happy sewing!

ALL ABOUT CORK FABRIC

Cork is used for so much more than mere bottle stoppers! It has become an invaluable component in a variety of products, such as flooring, wall coverings, yoga and sports equipment, home decor items, shoes, gift items, and even cork fabric.

Cork fabric is a versatile and unique material that is used to make bags, wallets, and accents on clothing, craft projects, appliqué, embroidery, and even upholstery. It feels much like high-quality leather and vinyl because it is soft, smooth, and pliable, but it's much easier to cut and sew. It is an amazing alternative to leather or vinyl because it's sustainable, washable, stain-resistant, durable, antimicrobial, and hypoallergenic. Cork fabric is not hard or brittle like the traditional cork sheets from the craft store. You'll be amazed how easy it is to work with and how forgiving it can be.

This high-quality fabric is a natural product made primarily in Mediterranean countries

such as Portugal, Spain, Morocco, and France. It is produced from the bark of the cork oak tree, which is harvested by experts in order to protect the tree. Once the cork is harvested from the cork oak, it's stacked on concrete pallets and left to dry for a minimum of six months. After it is fully dried, the cork is boiled and steamed for sterilization, flattening, and elasticity. Heat and pressure are applied to press the cork into blocks. The blocks are later shaved into thin sheets. These thin cork sheets are sealed with a nontoxic sealant and adhered to a fabric support backing (see Shopping for Cork and Related Materials, page 8). Because of this simple and natural production process, cork fabric retains all the qualities of raw cork!

There are numerous benefits to using this eco-friendly fabric that you'll learn to appreciate as you apply cork to a variety of projects for you and your home.

shopping for cork and related materials

There are several factors to consider when shopping for cork fabric, including quality, color, size, price, and how it will be used.

QUALITY

There are two main qualities of cork fabric: Touch and Touch Pro.

Touch features a coagulated fabric backing made of 35% polyester and 65% cotton. It is suitable for craft projects or items that won't have much day-to-day use. You cannot iron Touch cork fabric, and it may fade and show abrasion over time. It is an affordable option if you're trying cork for the first time or only need a small amount for a project.

Touch Pro features a textile backing made of 15.5% polyester, 29.5% cotton, and 55% polyurethane. It has a higher-quality cork than Touch cork fabric and is durable and long-lasting. For all the projects in this book, I recommend using Touch Pro–quality cork fabric. Your projects will have a more professional, long-lasting finish if you use good-quality cork fabric.

SIZE

Most cork fabric is either 27″ or 54″ wide and is sold by the inch, by the yard, or in specified sizes that are commonly used in sewing projects.

COLOR

Cork fabric is sold in a variety of colors, textures, and prints. A growing selection of cork fabric is available on my website (see Resources, page 126). Interestingly, the color of the cork fabric backing is often very different from the front.

PRICE

The price of cork fabric is reflected by the amount of time it takes to produce. The life cycle of cork fabric begins with the cork oak tree. It takes 25 years for a cork oak tree to begin producing cork, and the trunk of the tree needs to reach a specific circumference before it can be harvested. The first and second harvests produce material with a structure that is too hard and not of suitable quality to be manufactured. Each time the bark is harvested, the tree cannot be harvested again for another 9 years. Because of the length of time it takes to produce cork fabric, it is fairly expensive and is often referred to as *cork leather*.

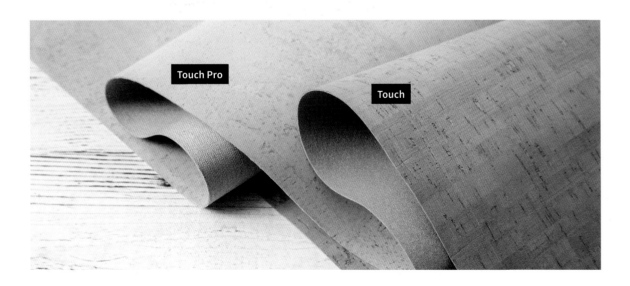

Touch Pro

Touch

The Benefits of Cork Fabric

- **Easy to cut and sew:** You don't need any special tools or equipment to sew cork fabric.

- **Lightweight:** Air accounts for 50 percent of cork's volume, making it ideal for bags and laptop carriers.

- **Easy to maintain and clean:** Just wipe it clean with soap and water.

- **Water- and stain-resistant:** Cork cells contain suberin and cerin, waxy substances that function as barriers to liquids. Resistant to moisture, cork fabric is very durable and does not deteriorate over time.

- **Long-lasting and durable:** Cork ages without deteriorating, mainly due to its resistance to moisture. Cork cells are packed closely together in radial rows; this honeycomb structure makes cork extremely durable and abrasion-resistant. Because of its structure and elasticity, cork is able to adapt to variations in temperature and pressure.

- **Hypoallergenic:** Cork is not allergy-proof, but it is very unlikely to cause an allergic reaction. This material does not absorb dust, making it a clean, safe material to sew. It is very gentle on your skin.

- **Soft:** Cork fabric feels like good-quality leather because it's soft, smooth, and pliable. It's not hard or brittle.

- **Unique:** No two pieces of cork fabric are alike.

- **100 percent sustainable and vegan:** The cork oak is the only tree in the world that can have its bark removed and survive, thus making the harvesting of cork 100 percent sustainable. The same tree can be harvested every 9 years. Some trees have been harvested for over 200 years! The best part of harvesting and producing cork is that everything is transformed into a final product. No part of the raw material goes to waste. And cork doesn't contain any animal products, which makes it a vegan material!

PAIRING CORK WITH FABRIC AND INTERFACING

For most projects, cork is used as an accent rather than as a main fabric. For the best results when choosing a complementary main fabric, pair cork fabric with woven fabrics such as quilt-weight cotton, canvas, waxed canvas, linen, or denim. Because cork fabric has a woven backing, it pairs well with other woven fabrics. Both cork and woven fabrics don't have a lot of natural stretch so they are easy to sew together. Avoid pairing cork with knit fabrics because knits tend to stretch in every direction.

Regardless of the type of woven fabric you choose, it should be stabilized with interfacing to establish a weight similar to the cork fabric you are using. Without adding interfacing, your woven fabric will not have the support it needs to pair up with cork. Also, it can be difficult for your sewing machine to sew through the variance of thicknesses.

Keep in mind that you might need to add different amounts and different weights of interfacing to the various fabrics suitable for sewing with cork. For example, quilt-weight cotton needs more interfacing than eight-ounce duck canvas. A general rule of thumb for using different interfacings is to start by applying an all-purpose midweight woven fusible

interfacing as a base layer to the wrong side of your main fabric. Then test the stability of the main fabric by aligning it with the cork and check to see that they have the same relative weight and stiffness. If the main fabric doesn't match the weight of the cork fabric, you might want to add another layer of fusible interfacing, or even a layer of fleece batting or foam, directly over the initial interfacing layer. See Resources (page 126) for some examples of fusible fleece batting and fusible foam.

TIP

Avoid using nonwoven interfacing because it behaves like paper. It tends to permanently crack and crease after it's fused. On the other hand, woven interfacing behaves like fabric; it doesn't detract from the natural drape and hand of the fabric to which it is fused.

Interfacing cork fabric is not necessary unless your pattern specifically requires extra stabilization. If you feel you need more stability, add a layer of fleece batting or foam to the project. If it is a pattern designed specifically for cork fabric, it will indicate whether you need any interfacing, foam, or fleece layers.

helpful sewing tools and notions

There are several tools and notions that make working with cork easy and the results more professional looking. You will also be using purse hardware to add a professional touch to many of the projects.

CUTTING TOOLS

If you plan to cut a lot of cork fabric, I suggest you purchase a rotary cutter and pair of scissors that you designate specifically for cutting cork. This will help keep your fabric-designated rotary cutter and scissors sharp.

TIP
Once you start working with cork fabric, you might want to consider purchasing a digital cutting machine, such as the Brother ScanNCut or Silhouette Cameo, for appliqué and cutwork designs. Be sure to test cut before cutting entire designs on cork fabric. When the blade and cutting mat are new, I recommend a blade depth of ten, cut pressure of five, and cut speed of one.

GLUE AND ADHESIVES

A variety of adhesives are useful to have on hand. Use basting tape or fabric glue for holding seams, positioning pockets and zippers, and creating straps. Temporary spray adhesive works great for holding cork appliqués, interfacings, and straps in place before and as you sew. Hot glue is a very strong adhesive suitable for cork craft projects. I would not recommend sewing through hot glue because it cools into a plastic that might break your needle. Permanent glue such as E6000 works well for applying embellishments (such as rhinestones) or hardware (such as a purse frame) to cork fabric.

MARKING TOOLS

Air-soluble fabric pens and pencils or tailor's chalk in a wheel or pencil can be used to trace patterns on the wrong side of cork fabric. A leather pen works well if you need to mark the right side of the cork fabric, but test the pen first on a scrap because the markings don't always rub off certain cork colors or textures.

PURSE HARDWARE

Purse hardware such as rivets, purse feet, and metal handles can make your bags stronger and add a professional touch. Add rivets to stabilize seams and straps on bags made with cork. Use purse feet to protect the bottom of your cork bags from rubbing against surfaces, and use metal handle hardware to attach handles and straps rather than sewing them directly to your bag.

Common purse hardware includes D-rings, swivel hooks, slider buckles, O-rings, and magnetic snaps.

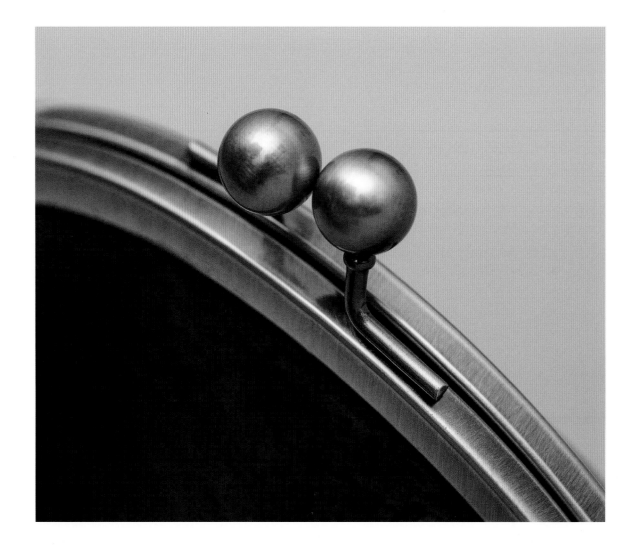

NEEDLES

It is a good idea to start each project with a new needle. Microtex needles size 80/12 or 90/14 have a narrow shaft and a very thin, sharp point, making them ideal for sewing cork fabric. Universal needles size 80/12 work well, too.

PRESSER FEET

A Teflon foot, walking foot, and compensating foot are all designed to help sewing machines glide through layers of cork easily. Every machine behaves differently, so it is important to test stitches with different presser feet to find the one that works best with your machine.

SEWING CLIPS

Since pins leave permanent holes in cork fabric and binder clips may leave impressions because of their strong pressure, I recommend using sewing clips to hold together seams.

THREAD

Generally, 40- to 50-weight all-purpose thread is suitable for seaming, topstitching, and appliqué. My personal favorite is Superior's So Fine! 50-weight polyester thread. It's a smooth, strong, lint-free, and matte-finish thread that works beautifully for many cork applications. If you prefer more defined topstitching or decorative work on top of cork, I'd recommend Superior's So Fine! 30-weight thread for a bolder stitch.

TURNING TOOLS

A turning tool helps you turn fabric right or wrong side out so you can press seams, points, and curves without tearing the fabric; it also helps press a good crease in a finished project. These multipurpose tools are also used to turn pockets, flaps, and bag bottoms. The pointed end can even be used to guide fabric while sewing.

working with cork fabric

Sewing with cork is no more difficult than sewing most fabrics. Practice helps, so it is always a good idea to sew a seam and topstitch on a scrap of the cork you plan to use before you start the actual project.

SEAMING, TOPSTITCHING, AND EDGE FINISHING

For seaming and piecing, use a ½″-wide seam allowance, unless otherwise noted, and a short stitch length of 2.5–3 mm. Topstitching requires a longer stitch length: 3–4 mm stitches per inch.

When sewing through multiple layers, lower the machine's tension and foot pressure. Most home sewing machines can generally sew through up to four layers of cork—or two layers of cork and two layers of fleece or foam—at a time.

Cork fabric does not fray, so there is no need to finish the edges. If you prefer, you can use seam sealant or leather edge paint to coat the raw edges for a smooth, sealed look.

HOW TO MAKE AND ATTACH BINDING

The following steps explain my favorite bias or straight-binding technique. However, you are welcome to use your own technique! The binding in this example is cut from 2½″-wide bias strips that finish at ½″ wide on the finished side of the project. If you prefer narrower or wider binding, cut the strips accordingly.

1 **For straight-grain binding**, cut the strips from selvage to selvage. Refer to Steps 5–7 (page 18) for joining. **For bias binding**, cut a square of fabric in half diagonally to yield 2 triangles. The size of square to cut is specified in the project directions.

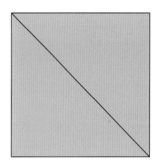

2 With right sides together, sew the triangles together on a short side with a ¼″ seam allowance, as shown. Make sure the 90° angles of the triangles are opposite each other. Press the seam open.

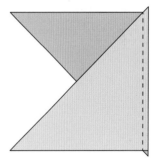

3 Mark and then cut 2½″ strips (or your desired width) on the bias edge of the fabric.

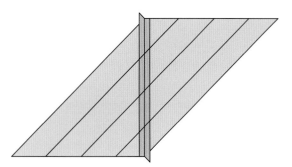

4 Join the strips by placing the angled ends right sides together, perpendicular to each other. Offset the ends ¼″ and sew. Press the seams open.

5 For straight-grain binding, place the ends right sides together, perpendicular to each other. Sew a diagonal seam from corner to corner.

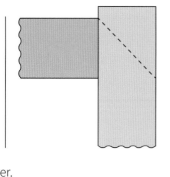

6 Trim the seam allowance to ¼″. Press the seam open.

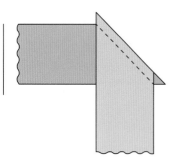

7 Continue to make one long strip.

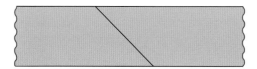

8 For straight-grain binding, cut one end at a 45° angle. (On bias-cut strips, the ends are already at an angle.) Fold the angled end of the binding ½″ to the wrong side, press, and trim the excess fabric even with the side.

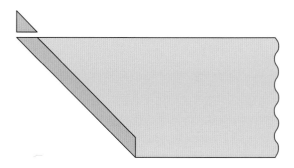

9 With wrong sides together, press the binding strip in half lengthwise.

10 Place the angled end of the binding on the back of the item being bound, matching the raw edges. Begin sewing about 4″ from the beginning end of the binding with a ¼″ seam allowance.

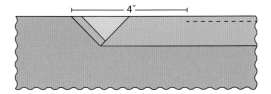

11 To miter the corners, refer to How to Miter Corners for a Bound Edge (at right).

12 When you're approximately 2″ from the beginning of the binding, trim the end of the binding so that it overlaps the angled edge and reaches to just before the starting point of the stitching. After trimming, tuck the tail end of binding into the angled beginning. Clip in place. Resume stitching the remainder of the seam.

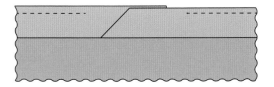

13 Fold and press the binding to the opposite side of the seam allowance, covering the raw edge, and clip in place. Topstitch the binding in place ⅛″ from the edge.

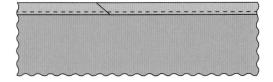

HOW TO MITER CORNERS FOR A BOUND EDGE

1 Stop stitching ¼″ from the corner and back-stitch to lock the stitches. Fold the binding away from the item being bound, creating a 45° angle.

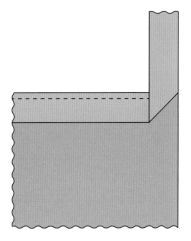

2 Fold the binding down, aligning the raw edges of the binding and the item being bound. The fold should be even with the top edge. Starting at the top edge, continue to stitch the binding in place with a ¼″ seam allowance. Repeat for each remaining corner.

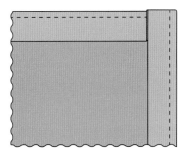

PRESSING

There usually is no need to press cork because it doesn't crease, and an iron won't have much effect on cork due to its thickness. However, if you wish or need to press cork fabric, you can iron quality Touch Pro cork on either side with a steam iron. Steam will make the cork fabric relax and stretch. A pressing cloth is not necessary because cork is an all-natural material that does not melt. Let the fabric cool before sewing.

CLEANING AND MAINTENANCE

Cork is easy to clean and is a low-maintenance material. Most cork fabric has been treated with Scotchgard by the manufacturer to protect it from stains, dirt, and water. To clean cork, periodically wipe it with soap and water. Lay your cork project flat to dry, or hang it upside down so the water doesn't pool in the bottom of your bag.

HOW TO USE THE PATTERNS

Several patterns are provided in the back of this book. Trace them to create templates you can use to mark and cut the fabric. The materials list for each project indicates if a pattern is needed, and if so, how many and which ones. The cutting instructions further indicate how many template shapes to cut and from which fabrics. The circle patterns are stacked one inside the other; you only need to trace the size you need, but be sure to write the size inside the traced circle so you don't mistakenly use the wrong size.

To use the patterns in this book, follow these steps:

1 Smooth tracing paper or baking parchment paper over the desired pattern. Use a marker to trace around the outside *and* around any interior cutout sections (the alphabet and reverse appliqué arrows in particular) within the body of the pattern.

2 Once all the markings are traced, cut out the template with paper scissors.

3 If you know you will be using the templates several times, you might want to trace them onto card stock or heavier paper so they are easier to trace around.

4 Write the name of the template and how many fabric pieces to cut directly on the traced template. This helps avoid confusion later!

MAKING THE PROJECTS

If you are new to using cork fabric, making the projects in this book will teach you how to incorporate cork into your sewing repertoire. The difficulty level of the various projects assumes you have a basic understanding of sewing, but the instructions have been written as beginner friendly as possible.

Once you branch out beyond the projects on the following pages, I recommend you use a pattern specifically written for cork fabric to achieve quality, long-lasting results. All Sallie Tomato patterns are written to accommodate a variety of materials, including cork fabric.

A few things to know before you start:

• To make all the featured projects, you will need a sewing machine, needles, scissors, and other basic sewing supplies. Any specific supplies beyond the basics are listed at the beginning of the instructions for each project.

• All cork yardage is for 27˝-wide cork, unless otherwise noted. It is carefully calculated to use almost every bit of the cork, leaving minimal left over. Add extra if you are worried about cutting errors. Be sure to save your scraps!

• Unless otherwise noted, all projects are sewn with 40- or 50-weight sewing thread.

• All seam allowances are ½˝ wide unless otherwise noted.

• Lining fabric is usually 44˝–45˝ wide. I recommend quilt-weight cotton, linen, or another lightweight woven for the lining fabric.

• There is no need to prewash cork fabric because it doesn't shrink and should only be cleaned when needed.

• The instructions for each project indicate the recommended width for seaming and topstitching.

bags

There are so many styles, features, and fun purse hardware pieces that can be incorporated into a bag. I've thoughtfully designed these projects to show off your cork fabric and allow for easy stitching on any standard sewing machine.

Fabrics: Cork Fabric by Sallie Tomato for exterior panels; Amalfi Herb Garden by Rifle Paper Co. for Cotton + Steel for lining

SKILL LEVEL: BEGINNER

Finished purse:
7½˝ wide × 7˝ high × 2˝ deep

FRAMED CLUTCH PURSE

This framed clutch is quick to make and perfect for keeping small items organized in a larger bag or backpack. It is fabulous on its own as a lightweight purse for those days when you don't want to carry a large bag.

materials

Cork (27″ wide): ¼ yard for exterior panels

Lining: ¼ yard

6″ purse frame

Permanent glue

Sewing clips

Turning tool

Flat-head screwdriver

cutting

Refer to How to Use the Patterns (page 20) to make templates using the patterns.

Templates: Make a template using the Framed Clutch Purse body pattern (page 120).

Cork: Cut 2 pieces using the template.

Lining: Cut 2 pieces using the template.

CONSTRUCTION

Seam allowances are ½″ unless otherwise noted.

prepare the exterior

1 With right sides together, align all edges of the exterior panels. Sew the side and bottom edges, starting and stopping ½″ from the upper edge. Make sure to backstitch.

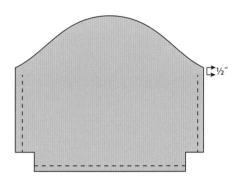

2 Create a boxed bottom at each bottom corner. With right sides together, match the bottom seam with the adjacent side seam. Sew, making sure to backstitch at each end. Stitch a second seam, ¼″ away from the first and toward the corner, for reinforcement. Trim the excess fabric at the corner. Repeat for the other bottom corner. Leave the bag exterior wrong side out.

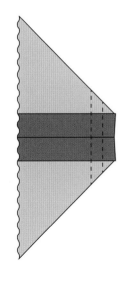

prepare the lining

Make the lining, following the steps for the exterior panels, but leave a 4″ opening in one of the side seams for turning. Turn the lining right side out.

attach the lining and exterior

1 With right sides together, place the prepared lining inside the prepared exterior. Align the side seams and upper edges.

2 Sew together ½″ from the top edges.

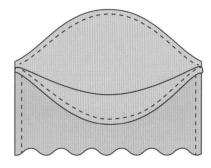

3 Using sharp scissors, cut slits along the upper edge to help shape the curved edge. Be careful not to cut through the stitching.

4 Turn the clutch right side out through the opening in the lining. Use a turning tool to smooth out the upper curve and poke out the bottom corners.

5 Topstitch the upper curved edge ⅛″ from the finished edge.

6 Fold the clutch in half lengthwise to find and mark the center of the upper edges.

attach the clutch to the frame

1 Apply a thin line of glue to the inside of each channel of the purse frame, from one hinge to the other.

2 Match each center top of the clutch with the center top of the purse frame. Push the upper edge of the clutch into the channel of the frame.

TIP
A flat-head screwdriver helps push the fabric up into the channel. Be careful not to scratch the purse frame!

3 Use sewing clips to hold the top edge of the clutch in the frame. Allow the glue to dry for 24 hours before using your clutch.

TIP
If your sewing clips are too small to hold the purse
frame in place, use clothespins or large binder clips.

CROSS-BODY BAG

This cross-body bag is perfect for everyday trips or travel. The front flap makes it easy to access your essentials while keeping them safe. You'll learn how to make darts, a cork flap, and an adjustable strap while sewing this bag together.

SKILL LEVEL: INTERMEDIATE

Finished bag:
9˝ wide × 7˝ high × 2½˝ deep

Fabrics: Surface Navy Cork Fabric by Sallie Tomato for flap, tassel, and strap; Mesh with Me Worn by April Rhodes for Art Gallery Fabrics for exterior fabric. Choose something from your stash for the lining.

materials

Cork (27″ wide): ¼ yard for flap, tassel, and adjustable strap

Main fabric: ¼ yard for bag exterior panels

Lining: ⅓ yard

Fusible fleece: ¼ yard

½″ hardware: 2 D-rings, 1 slider buckle, and 2 swivel hooks

1½″ O-ring

Magnetic snap

Hot glue gun and glue

Double-sided basting tape

Sewing clips

cutting

Refer to How to Use the Patterns (page 20) to make templates using the patterns.

Templates: Make a template using the 6½″ circle pattern (page 119).

Cork

- Cut 1 flap 7″ × 7″.
- Cut 1 tassel 4″ × 4″.
- Cut 2 tassel connectors ½″ × 1½″.
- Cut 2 strap connectors ½″ × 1½″.
- Cut 2 adjustable strap pieces 1″ × 27″.

Main fabric: Cut 2 exterior panels 11″ × 9″.

Lining

- Cut 1 flap 7″ × 7″.
- Cut 2 exterior panels 11″ × 9″.

Fusible fleece

- Cut 1 flap 6″ × 6″.
- Cut 2 exterior panels 11″ × 9″.

CONSTRUCTION

Seam allowances are ½″ unless otherwise noted.

prepare the flap

1 Center and fuse the fusible fleece on the wrong side of the lining flap piece.

> **TIP**
> The fusible fleece is smaller than the flap piece, so most of the fleece will be inside the seam stitching. This helps reduce bulk.

2 Mark the center on the bottom edge of the cork flap and the lining flap.

3 On the right side of the lining flap, install one-half of a magnetic snap according to the manufacturer's instructions. The snap should be centered and 1½″ up from the bottom edge. Fuse a scrap of fusible fleece over the wrong side of the snap to prevent the prongs from rubbing against the fabric.

4 Make the tassel (see Tassel Tutorial, page 105). Attach one tassel connector to the tassel as instructed. Note that you need to slide the O-ring over the end of the connector instead of a swivel clip, as indicated in the tassel-making instructions. Slide the remaining tassel connector over the opposite side of the O-ring and baste the ends together.

5 Use the 6½″ circle template (page 119) to round both bottom corners of the cork flap and lining flap.

6 On the top edge of each flap piece, mark ½″ in from each side and 2″ down from the top. Draw a diagonal line between the markings on each side. Cut along the diagonal lines to create tapered edges.

7 With right sides together, center the raw edge of the tassel connector on the bottom edge of the cork flap. Stitch in place using a ¼″ seam allowance.

8 With right sides together, align all edges of the cork flap and the lining flap. Stitch, leaving a 3″ opening on the top edge. Make sure the tassel is out of the way of the stitching. Trim the seam allowance to ¼″. Cut out small notches along the curves and trim the corners diagonally.

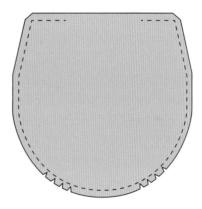

9 Turn the flap right side out through the opening. Topstitch the side and bottom edges ⅛″ and ¼″ from the edges. Leave the top edge unsewn. Tuck in the raw edges of the opening and use sewing clips to hold them in place. Set aside the assembled flap.

prepare the exterior

1 Fuse the fusible fleece to the wrong side of each exterior panel piece.

2 Use the 6½″ circle template to round the bottom corners of each exterior panel piece, as shown in Prepare the Flap, Step 5 (page 30).

3 Install the remaining half of the magnetic snap, centered 3½″ down from the top edge and on the right side of one main panel. Fuse a scrap of fusible fleece against the wrong side of the snap to prevent the prongs from rubbing against the fabric.

CREATE THE DARTS

1 Fold and match the right edge with the bottom edge of one exterior panel piece, right sides together. On the folded bottom corner, mark 2″ up and ½″ in from the fold. Draw a diagonal line between the markings. Sew on the diagonal line to create a dart. Press the dart toward the center.

3 Repeat the same process to create darts on the remaining exterior panel.

4 Fold each exterior panel piece with right sides together so that the side edges meet in the center of the panel, as shown. On each folded edge, mark 2″ down and ½″ in from the top edge. Draw a diagonal line between the markings. Sew on each diagonal line to create the top darts. Press the darts toward the center.

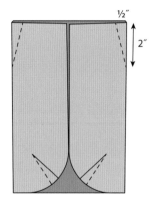

2 Repeat to create a dart on the other bottom corner.

attach the flap

1 Adhere double-sided basting tape to the lining side of the assembled flap along the unsewn top edge.

2 With right sides up, position the unsewn edge of the flap 1½″ down from the top edge of the exterior panel without the magnetic snap. Press down to adhere the flap in place. To attach the flap and close the opening, topstitch ⅛″ and ¼″ from the edge.

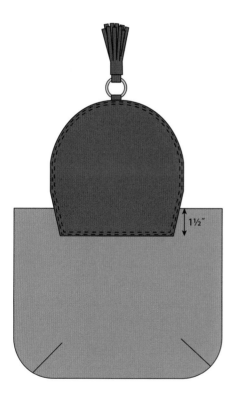

attach the strap connectors

1 Slide one D-ring over the end of each strap connector so that the D-ring is in the center and the flat side of the hardware is against the wrong side of the connector. Fold each connector in half, matching the short raw edges.

2 With right sides together, position one strap connector on each side of one exterior panel, 1″ down from the top edge and aligning the raw edges. Use sewing clips to hold in place.

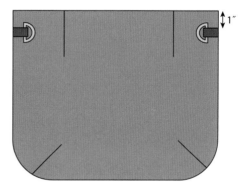

prepare the lining

1 Use the 6½″ circle template to round the bottom corners of each lining panel, as shown in Prepare the Flap, Step 5 (page 30).

2 Repeat the same process as for the exterior panels to create darts on the bottom corners and top edge of each lining panel.

assemble the bag

1 With right sides together, align the exterior panels and stitch along the sides and bottom edge. Make sure the hardware, flap, and tassel are out of the way of the stitching. Leave the panels wrong side out.

2 Repeat the same process to sew the lining pieces together, but leave a 3″ opening along the bottom edge. Turn the lining right side out.

3 Insert the assembled lining into the assembled exterior with right sides together, tucking the flap down and between the exterior and lining. Align the side seams and pin them together. Sew around the entire top edge.

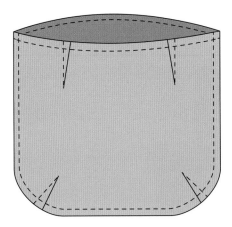

4 Turn the assembled bag right side out by pushing the exterior and lining through the opening in the lining.

5 Hand sew or topstitch the opening closed, ⅛″ from the edges.

6 Smooth the lining down into the exterior. Topstitch ¼″ from the top edge. Set the bag aside.

make and attach the adjustable strap

1 Join the adjustable strap pieces by placing the short ends right sides together, perpendicular to each other and overlapping the ends. Sew at a 45° angle from edge to edge. Trim the excess seam allowance to ¼″ wide. Press the seam open. Topstitch ⅛″ from each side of the seam.

2 Fold the assembled adjustable strap in half lengthwise with wrong sides together. Topstitch ⅛″ from each long side.

3 With right sides up, thread one end of the strap over the center bar of the slider buckle. Fold the end of strap 1″ to the underside. Topstitch the end of the strap to itself, ⅛″ and ¼″ from the end.

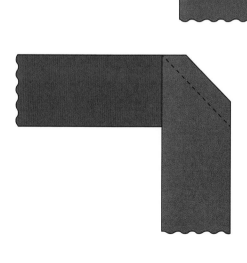

4 With the wrong side up, thread the end without the slider buckle through a swivel hook until it's approximately 6″ from the slider buckle. Thread the end of the strap over the center bar of the slider buckle again.

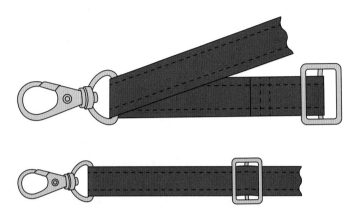

5 To complete the adjustable strap, make sure the strap isn't twisted and thread the end through the remaining swivel hook.

6 Fold the end of the strap 1″ to the underside. Topstitch the end of the strap to itself, ⅛″ and ¼″ from the end.

7 Clip one hook to each ring on the bag.

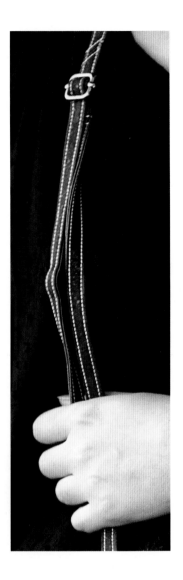

SHOPPING TOTE

This sturdy tote features two colors of cork fabric—one for the pockets and another for the straps—and your favorite quilting cotton or canvas fabric for the exterior panels! The deep exterior pockets are ideal for storing items you want to keep handy and secure.

Fabrics: Surface Natural and Army Green Cork Fabric by Sallie Tomato for straps and pocket; Monstera by Rifle Paper Co. for Cotton + Steel for exterior panels; Sprinkle (Summer Camp) by Sarah Watts for Cotton + Steel for lining

materials

You'll use almost every bit of the cork yardage, except for a few scraps left over in case you want to make different-colored tassels (page 105) to embellish your tote!

Main cork (27″ wide): 14″ for front and back pockets, base, magnetic snap accent, and optional tassels

Accent cork (54″ wide): 9″ for handles and tassels

Main fabric: ½ yard for exterior panels

Lining: ⅔ yard

Lightweight woven fusible interfacing (20″ wide): ⅞ yard

Fusible fleece: ½ yard

Firm stabilizer: ¼ yard

Magnetic snap

Fabric glue *or* **double-sided basting tape**

Small rivets: 4 *(optional)*

cutting

Refer to How to Use the Patterns (page 20) to make templates from the patterns.

Templates: Make templates using the 3½″ circle pattern (page 119) and the Shopping Tote magnetic snap accent pattern (page 120).

Main cork

- Cut 1 base 7″ × 14″.
- Cut 2 pockets 9″ × 11″.
- Cut 2 magnetic snap accents using the templates.
- Cut 1 tassel connector ½″ × 14″ *(optional)*.
- Cut 2 tassels 5″ × 3″ *(optional)*.

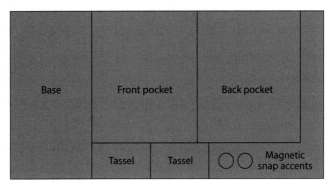

Cutting layout

Accent cork

- Cut 2 handles 3″ × 50″.
- Cut 1 tassel connector ½″ × 14″.
- Cut 2 tassels 5″ × 3″.

Main fabric: Cut 1 strip 14″ × width of fabric; subcut into 2 exterior panels 14″ × 20″.

Lining

- Cut 1 strip 14″ × width of fabric; subcut into 2 interior panels 14″ × 20″.
- Cut 1 base 6″ × 13″.

Lightweight woven fusible interfacing: Cut 2 strips 14″ × width of fabric; subcut into 2 pieces 14″ × 20″ for the exterior panels.

Fusible fleece: Cut 1 strip 14″ × width of fabric; subcut into 2 pieces 14″ × 20″ for the exterior panels.

Firm stabilizer: Cut 1 base 6″ × 13″.

CONSTRUCTION

Seam allowances are ½˝ unless otherwise noted.

prepare the exterior

1 Fuse the fusible interfacing to the wrong side of the main fabric panels. Repeat to fuse the fusible fleece directly over the interfacing.

2 Fold one of the 9˝ edges of each cork pocket ½˝ to the wrong side; topstitch ¼˝ from the fold for the pocket's top edge.

3 Apply fabric glue or double-sided basting tape along the wrong side of the side and bottom edges of each pocket. Center one pocket on each exterior panel along the bottom edge, 5½˝ in from each side edge, as shown. Match the bottom raw edges and press down to adhere the pockets in place; topstitch ¼˝ from the sides and bottom edge.

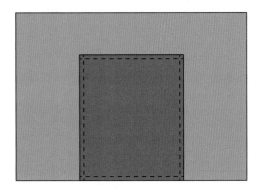

ATTACH THE HANDLES

1 Apply fabric glue or double-sided basting tape on the wrong side of the long edges of each handle. Fold each long edge to the center and press down to adhere in place. Topstitch ⅛″ from the center on both edges.

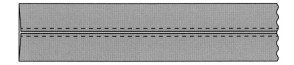

2 On each handle, measure and mark 13″ from the ends. Fold the center portion of the handle in half lengthwise and use sewing clips to hold the folds in place. Topstitch ⅛″ from the folds and across the 13″ marks.

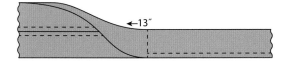

3 On each handle, measure and mark 11½″ from the ends. Apply fabric glue or double-sided basting tape on the wrong side of the handle ends, up to the 11½″ marks.

4 Position one handle on each exterior panel, with the raw edges on the bottom. Position the handle 4½″ in from the side on the bottom edge and 5½″ in from the side on the top edge. Press down to adhere in place.

TIP

Cork fabric cannot be pinned. It would be difficult to clip the handles in place for this step—which is why fabric glue or double-sided basting tape are handy notions to keep in your sewing room for working with cork!

5 Topstitch each handle in place ⅛″ from the edges. Start at the bottom of the bag, topstitch up one long side edge, pivot and stitch across at the 11½″ mark, and continue stitching down the other long side of the handle. Insert a small rivet ½″ down from each 11½″ mark according to the manufacturer's instructions, if desired.

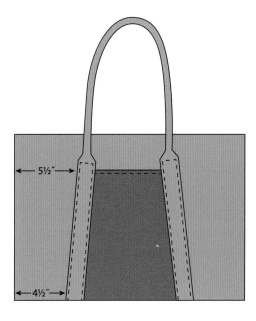

ATTACH THE CORK BASE

1 Mark the center on each side of the cork base by folding it in half from each direction.

2 Use the 3½″ circle template to mark the corners of the cork base and the stabilizer. Trim on the marks to round the corners.

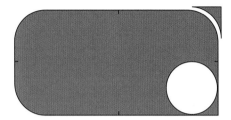

TIP

The firm stabilizer base is cut smaller than the cork base so it doesn't get sewn into the seam allowance in an upcoming step. The firmness of the stabilizer helps prevent the bottom of the bag from sagging over time.

3 Apply fabric glue or double-sided basting tape to one side of the stabilizer base. Center the stabilizer base on the wrong side of the cork base. Press down to adhere. Topstitch the stabilizer base in place ¼″ from the edges.

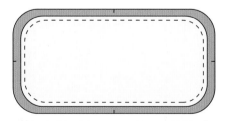

4 Pin the exterior panels with right sides together, aligning all edges. Stitch the sides with a ½″ seam allowance. Mark the center front and back on the top and bottom edges.

5 With right sides together, match the center marks on the base with the center marks on the bottom edge of the exterior panels. Attach sewing clips to hold the centers together. Then continue to place clips around the entire bottom. *Double-check that the base is clipped to the bottom edge of the exterior and the long edges of the base are aligned with the outer pockets.*

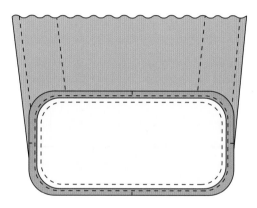

TIP

Use lots of sewing clips to hold the layers together! More clips will help prevent your fabric from shifting or puckering while you sew.

6 Sew around the entire bottom edge, stitching close to the stabilizer but not through it. Stop stitching with your needle down to readjust as needed along the curves.

TIP

If you're having trouble with this step, use scissors to cut small notches from the curved edges of the base to help the cork flex. Do not cut into the edge of the cork more than ¼″ or you might cut beyond the seamline. Take your time—you've got this!

7 Leave the assembled exterior wrong side out and set aside.

prepare the lining

ADD THE MAGNETIC SNAP

1 Mark the center of both magnetic snap-accent pieces. Install one-half of a magnetic snap on each piece. Insert from the right side and fuse a scrap of interfacing on the wrong side to prevent the prongs from rubbing against the fabric. Refer to the manufacturer's instructions for more information.

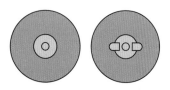

2 With right sides up, position one magnetic snap accent on each lining panel, centered 1½″ down from the top edge. Carefully topstitch ⅛″ around the edge of each magnetic snap accent.

TIP

A zipper foot helps you stitch close to the edge of the accent piece!

ATTACH THE LINING BASE

1 Mark the center on each side of the lining base by folding it in half from each direction.

2 Use the 3½″ circle template to round the corners of the lining base, as shown in Attach the Cork Base, Step 2 (page 42).

3 Pin the lining panels right sides together and align all edges. Sew the side edges together. Mark the center front and back along the top and bottom edges.

4 With right sides together, match the center marks on the base with the center marks on the bottom edge of the lining. Use pins to hold the matching centers together. Continue to pin around the entire bottom. *Double-check that the base is pinned to the bottom edge of the lining and the long edges of the base are aligned with the long edges of the lining.*

5 Sew around the entire bottom edge. Leave a 6″ opening for turning.

6 Trim the seam allowance to ¼″ wide. Turn the assembled lining right side out.

assemble the bag

ATTACH THE LINING AND EXTERIOR

1 Insert the assembled lining into the assembled exterior with right sides together, tucking the handles between the exterior and the lining. Match and pin the center marks and side seams on the top edge of the exterior and lining. Sew around the entire top edge.

2 Turn the assembled bag right side out through the opening in the lining.

3 Hand sew or topstitch the opening closed, ⅛″ from the edges.

4 Push the lining down into the exterior. Topstitch ⅜″ from the top edge.

make and attach the tassels

1 Make 2 tassels (see Tassel Tutorial, page 105). Attach one tassel to each end of the tassel connector.

2 Fold the tassel connector in half and wrap it around one side of the handle. Thread the tassels through the folded end of the tassel connector and pull tight to secure it on the handle.

Fabrics: Surface Light Pink Cork Fabric by Sallie Tomato for panels; Wind Observer (Fog) by Bonnie Christine for Art Gallery Fabrics for side panels and drawstring

TRENDY BUCKET BAG

Showcase your cork fabric by making this trendy bucket bag! The cork panels on the front and back of the bag add structure and stability, while the soft cork straps keep this bag lightweight and comfortable to carry. Pair your cork fabric with your favorite quilt cotton or canvas. In this project, you'll learn how to make a drawstring and slip pockets.

materials

Cork (27″ wide): 14″ for front and back panels, base, strap connectors, and shoulder strap

Main fabric: ½ yard for side panels, drawstring, and drawstring tab

Lining: ⅔ yard for lining and slip pockets

Fusible fleece: ½ yard

Firm stabilizer: ¼ yard

½″ grommets: 12

1″ O-rings: 2

Fabric glue *or* **double-sided basting tape**

cutting

Refer to How to Use the Patterns (page 20) to make templates from the patterns.

Templates: Make templates using the 5″ and 5½″ circle patterns (page 119).

Cork

- Cut 1 shoulder strap 2″ × width of fabric.
- Cut 1 front and 1 back panel 6½″ × 12″.
- Cut 1 base 8″ × 12″.
- Cut 2 strap connectors 2″ × 12″.

Shoulder strap					
Base	Front	Back		Strap connector	Strap connector

Cutting layout

Main fabric

- Cut 1 drawstring 1¾″ × width of fabric.
- Cut 2 side panels 12½″ × 12″.
- Cut 1 drawstring tab 4″ × 2½″.

Lining

- Cut 1 front and 1 back panel 6½″ × 12″.
- Cut 2 side panels 12½″ × 12″.
- Cut 2 pockets 6½″ × 12″.
- Cut 1 base 7″ × 11″.

Fusible fleece

- Cut 1 front and 1 back panel 6½″ × 12″.
- Cut 2 side panels 12½″ × 12″.

Firm stabilizer:

Cut 1 base 7″ × 11″.

CONSTRUCTION

Seam allowances are ½″ unless otherwise noted.

prepare the exterior

Fuse the fusible fleece to the wrong side of the cork front and back panels and exterior side panels.

MAKE THE STRAP CONNECTORS

1 On one short end of each strap connector, mark ¼″ in from each side and 1¼″ down from the top. Draw a diagonal line between the marks. Cut along the diagonal lines to create tapered ends.

TIP

By tapering the ends, you reduce bulk, making it easier to later conceal the raw end of the strap connector. This creates a more professional finish.

2 Apply fabric glue or double-sided basting tape down the center of each strap connector. Fold each long side of the connectors to the center with wrong sides together.

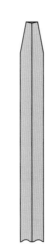

3 Thread the tapered end of each strap connector through an O-ring. Fold the tapered end 1¼″ to the wrong side.

4 Use a sewing clip to hold the fold. On the wrong side of each connector, apply fabric glue or double-sided basting tape down the center. Center the connectors on the right side of each exterior side panel, as shown. Align the bottom raw edges so the O-ring is at the top. Press down on each connector to adhere it in place. Top-stitch an ⅛″ seam from the edge, stopping approximately ¾″ from the top fold, stitching across, and continuing down the other side.

TIP

A zipper foot makes it easier to see where you are stitching, particularly when you want to stitch close to an edge.

ATTACH THE SIDE PANELS

1 With right sides together, sew the 12″ edges of the exterior side panels to the cork front panel. Press the seams to the side panels.

2 With right sides together, sew the remaining 12″ edges of the exterior side panels to the cork back panel. Press the seams to the side panels. See the tip (below) for optional topstitching.

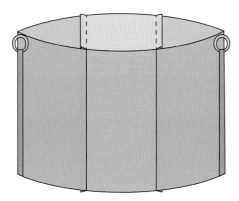

TIP

Pressing to the side panels reduces bulk, and topstitching the seam allowance ¼″ from the seam helps the cork lie flat. I find it's easier to topstitch the seams of the back panel with the wrong side out and when stitching slowly.

3 Measure and mark the centers of the front, back, and sides on the top and bottom edges.

ATTACH THE CORK BASE

1 Use the 5½″ circle template to round the corners of the cork base and the 5″ circle template to round the corners of the stabilizer base.

2 Refer to Shopping Tote, Attach the Cork Base, Steps 3–7 (pages 42 and 43) to attach the cork base to the bag.

prepare the slip pockets and lining

1 Fold and press each slip pocket in half lengthwise with wrong sides together to measure 6½″ × 6″. Topstitch ¼″ from the fold for the top edge of the pocket.

2 Position the pockets on the lining panels, aligning the side and bottom raw edges. Baste in place with a ¼″ seam allowance.

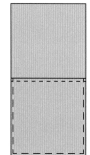

3 With right sides together, sew the 12″ edges of the lining side panels to the lining front panel. Start sewing at the top edge with a ½″ seam allowance; then gradually increase the seam allowance to ¾″ at the bottom. Trim the seam allowance to ¼″ and press to the front panel.

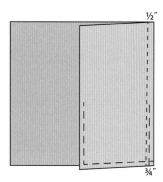

TIP
Gradually increasing the seam allowance in the lining seams will help the lining fit better inside the bag. This technique can be used with almost any bag pattern!

4 With right sides together, sew the 12″ edges of the lining side panels to the lining back panel. Increase the seam allowance to ¾″ as described in Step 3 (below left). Trim the seams and press to the back panel.

5 Measure and mark the centers of the front, back, and sides along the top and bottom edges of the lining.

6 Mark the center on each side of the lining base by folding it in half from each direction.

7 Use the 5″ circle template to round each of the 4 corners of the lining base, as shown in Shopping Tote, Attach the Cork Base, Step 2 (page 42).

8 With right sides together, match the center marks on the base with the center marks on the bottom edge of the lining. Use pins to hold the centers first. Continue to pin around the entire bottom. *Double-check that the base is pinned to the bottom edge of the lining and the long edges of the base are aligned with the front and back panels.*

9 Sew around the entire bottom edge with a ½″ seam allowance.

10 Turn the assembled lining right side out.

assemble the bag

ATTACH THE LINING AND EXTERIOR

1 Insert the lining into the assembled exterior with right sides together. Match the center marks and seams on the top edges of the lining and the exterior. Use sewing clips to hold in place. Sew the top edge, leaving a 6″ opening on one side of the panel for turning.

2 Turn the assembled bag right side out through the opening on the top edge. Fold the top raw edges so they are even with the top of the bag. Topstitch ⅛″ and ⅜″ from the top edge.

MAKE THE DRAWSTRING

1 Fold and press the ends of the drawstring ½″ to the wrong side. Fold and press the long edges to the center.

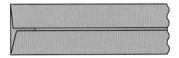

2 Fold and press in half again. The drawstring should measure about ⅜″ wide. Topstitch ⅛″ from the edges.

MAKE THE DRAWSTRING TAB

1 Press each long edge of the drawstring tab ¼″ to the wrong side.

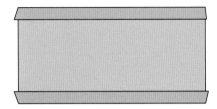

2 Press each long edge to the center so the tab is 1″ wide. Topstitch ⅛″ and ⅜″ from the long edges.

3 With right sides together, fold the tab in half, matching the raw edges. Sew together with a ¼″ seam allowance. Press the seam open.

4 Turn the tab right side out so the seam falls in the center of one side. Topstitch ¼″ from each side of the seam and set the drawstring tab aside.

INSTALL THE GROMMETS

1 Mark the placement of the grommets on the exterior. Measure so the center of the grommets is 1¼″ from the top edge. On the front and back cork panels, measure and mark 1½″ away from each seam. On each side panel, measure and mark 2″ away from each seam. Measure and mark 2″ toward the center from those marks.

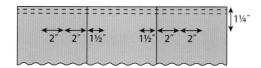

2 Install 12 grommets, one at each placement mark, according to the manufacturer's instructions.

TIP

You can use a grommet hole punch to cut the holes. Otherwise, use a seam ripper to start the hole; then use a pair of small scissors to cut the size of hole you need. Insert the grommets as you make the holes to prevent shifting.

3 Thread the drawstring through one of the middle grommets on the front of your bag. Continue by weaving the same end of the drawstring through all of the grommets, alternating from the inside to the outside of the bag. The end of the strap should come out through the other middle grommet on the front.

4 Thread each end of the drawstring through the channels of the drawstring tab.

5 Knot each end of the drawstring.

SHOULDER STRAP

1 Fold the shoulder strap in half lengthwise with wrong sides together. Topstitch ⅛″ from the long edges.

2 Thread the short end of the shoulder strap through one ring on the bag from the exterior side towards the lining side. Fold the end of the strap 1″ to the underside.

3 Topstitch the end of the strap to itself ⅛″ and ¼″ from the edge. Repeat for the opposite side of the strap and the other ring on the bag.

BASIC BACKPACK

This fabulous backpack is perfect as a hands-free purse, with plenty of pockets for storage. But it is also large enough to fit a standard notebook or binder, so it's great for students, too! Pair cork fabric with your favorite quilt cotton or canvas. This project will walk you through how to attach a zipper to cork fabric and how to make and attach bias binding to cover seam allowances.

Fabrics: Surface Army Green Cork Fabric by Sallie Tomato for pocket, gusset, and straps; Rosa (Natural) by Rifle Paper Co. for Cotton + Steel for front and back panels. Choose a lining fabric from your stash.

materials

There will be a bit of cork fabric left over—be sure to save it for some of the other smaller projects! Try using Sallie Tomato zippers by the yard for this project. You might want to note all the pockets: There is a flap pocket on the front exterior, a zipper pocket in the front exterior, and a slip pocket in the back lining!

Cork (27″ wide): ⅞ yard for front flap pocket, front zipper pocket, adjustable straps, strap connectors, handle, trim, and gussets

Main fabric: ½ yard for front and back exterior panels

Lining: 2 yards for front flap pocket, front zipper pocket, backpack lining, slip pocket, and gussets

Lightweight woven fusible interfacing (20″ wide): ¾ yard for front flap pocket and gusset

Fusible fleece: ⅜ yard

1″ hardware: 2 rectangle rings and 2 slider buckles

14″ zipper or longer

24″ double-slide zipper or longer

Tailor's chalk *or* **air-erasable marker**

Fabric glue *or* **double-sided basting tape**

Turning tool

Zipper foot

Metal snaps: 2 *(optional)*

cutting

Refer to How to Use the Patterns (page 20) to make templates from the patterns.

Templates: Make templates using the 3½″ and 6½″ circle patterns (page 119).

Cork

- Cut 1 strip 9″ × width of fabric; subcut 1 front pocket 9″ × 6″ and 1 front flap 9″ × 4″.
- Cut 3 adjustable straps 2″ × width of fabric.
- Cut 1 strip 2″ × width of fabric; subcut 1 handle 2″ × 12″, 1 trim 2″ × 12″, and 2 strap connectors 1″ × 3″.
- Cut 2 zipper gussets 3″ × 22″.
- Cut 1 bottom gusset 5″ × 25″.

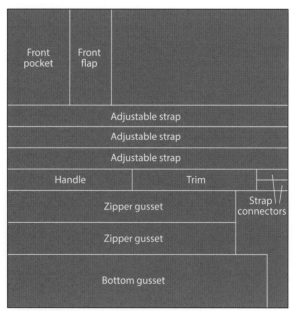

Cutting layout

Main fabric: Cut 1 front and 1 back exterior panel 12″ × 14″.

Lining

- Cut 1 front and 1 back panel 12″ × 14″.
- Cut 1 front pocket 9″ × 6″.
- Cut 1 front flap 9″ × 4″.
- Cut 1 front zipper pocket A 12″ × 10″.
- Cut 1 front zipper pocket B 12″ × 11″.
- Cut 1 slip pocket 12″ × 18″.
- Cut 2 zipper gussets 3″ × 22″.
- Cut 1 bottom gusset 5″ × 25″.
- Cut 1 bias binding square 20″ × 20″.

Lightweight woven fusible interfacing

- Cut 1 piece 9″ × 6″ for the front pocket.
- Cut 1 piece 9″ × 4″ for the front flap.
- Cut 2 pieces 3″ × 22″ for the zipper gusset.
- Cut 1 piece 5″ × 25″ for the bottom gusset.

Fusible fleece: Cut 2 pieces 12″ × 14″ for the exterior panels.

CONSTRUCTION

Seam allowances are ⅜″ unless otherwise noted.

prepare the front exterior panel

Fuse the fusible fleece to the wrong side of the front exterior panel.

MAKE THE FRONT FLAP POCKET

1 Fuse the interfacing to the wrong side of the lining front pocket and lining front flap.

2 Use the 3½″ circle template to round the 2 bottom corners of the lining front pocket, lining front flap, cork front pocket, and cork front flap.

3 Place the cork and fabric front-pocket pieces right sides together and stitch on all edges, leaving 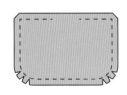 a 3″ opening on the top edge. Diagonally trim the top corners and notch the curves to reduce bulk in the seam.

4 Turn the front pocket right side out. Use a turning tool to smooth out the curves and  push out the corners. Tuck in the raw edges of the opening, making sure the top edge is even.

Press and steam the pocket flat. Topstitch ⅛″ and ⅜″ from the top edge.

TIP
You can iron and steam quality cork fabric without harming your fabric or your iron! The steam relaxes the seams and helps smooth out any creases caused by turning. Make sure to let your fabric cool before touching it because it can be very hot. Do not iron if using Touch-quality cork.

5 Place the front flap pieces right sides together and sew the side and bottom  edges, leaving the top edge unsewn. Notch the curves. Turn right side out and press flat. Topstitch ⅛″ and ⅜″ from the side and bottom edges.

6 Apply fabric glue or double-sided basting tape on the side and bottom edges of the front pocket lining. Center the front pocket, cork side up,

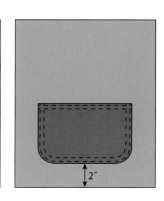

2″ up from the bottom edge of the front panel. Press down to adhere in place. Topstitch ⅛″ and ⅜″ from the side and bottom edges of the pocket.

7 Apply fabric glue or double-sided basting tape on the top raw edge of the cork side of the front flap. Center the front flap 1″ up from the front pocket,

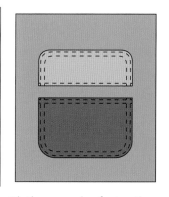

cork side down and with the raw edge facing the bottom, as shown. Press down to adhere the flap in place. Sew ⅛″ from the raw edge of the flap.

8 Fold the flap down over the seam. Press and steam it flat. Topstitch ⅛″ and ⅜″ from the top pressed edge.

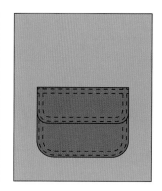

9 *Optional:* Attach one snap 1″ from each flap side and bottom edge according to the manufacturer's instructions. Repeat to attach the other half of the snap 1″ from each pocket side and top edge.

MAKING THE FRONT-PANEL ZIPPER POCKET

1 Measure and mark a horizontal line 4″ from the top edge of the front panel using tailor's chalk or an air-erasable marker. Cut on the line to divide the front panel into 2 pieces.

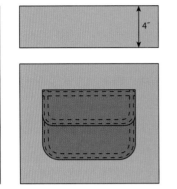

2 Center the 14″ or longer zipper on the top edge of the bottom exterior front panel with right sides together and the zipper pull on the left side, as shown. Position lining pocket A, right side down, over the zipper, with all top edges aligned. Using a zipper foot, sew with a ¼″ seam allowance through all the layers.

TIP

Using a zipper that is longer than the opening makes it easier to stitch the zipper in place without worrying about the zipper pull getting in the way of the needle or your presser foot.

3 Fold the lining and exterior panel away from the zipper so they are wrong sides together and press. Topstitch ¼″ from the seam.

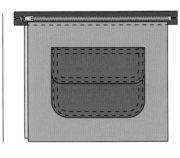

4 With right sides up, center the assembled bottom exterior front panel on top of lining pocket B, aligning the top 12″ edges. With right sides together, center the top exterior front panel over the assembled bottom front panel and align the top edges, including the zipper tape. Sew the layers together with a ¼″ seam allowance.

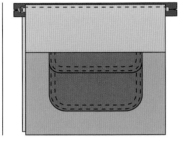

5 Fold only the top front panel away from the zipper and press. Topstitch ¼″ from the seam.

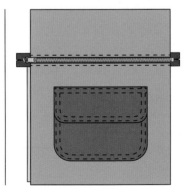

6 Sew the side and bottom edges of the zipper pocket together with a ¼″ seam allowance. Trim any excess pocket fabric and the zipper ends even with the edges of the front panel, making sure the zipper pull tab is within the seam allowance.

7 Measure the assembled front and make sure it is 14″ long. If necessary, trim the excess fabric from the top edge.

MAKE THE ADJUSTABLE STRAPS AND CONNECTORS

1 Slide one rectangle ring over the end of each strap connector so the rectangle ring is in the center. Fold each connector in half, matching the ends. Topstitch ⅛″ from the edges and approximately ½″ from the top fold. Set aside.

2 Follow Cross-Body Bag, Make and Attach the Adjustable Strap, Steps 1–3 (page 35). Cut the adjustable strap in half after completing Step 1.

prepare the exterior back panel

1 Fuse the fusible fleece panel to the wrong side of the exterior back panel.

2 With the wrong side of each adjustable strap facing up, position the raw ends of each strap 3″ down from the top and 2″ in from the sides of the exterior back panel. Stitch in place ⅛″ and ¼″ from the ends.

3 Position the ends of each strap connector on the bottom of the exterior back panel, 2″ in from each side. Stitch in place ⅛″ and ¼″ from the ends.

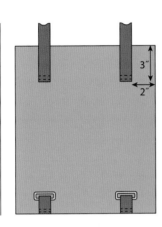

ATTACH THE HANDLE

1 Fold the handle in half lengthwise with wrong sides together. Topstitch ⅛″ from the long edges.

2 Position the handle in between the attached straps, with the ends even. Stitch in place ⅛″ and ¼″ from the ends.

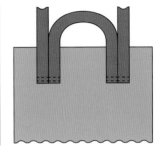

ATTACH THE TRIM

1 Fold the long edges of the trim to the center, wrong sides together. Topstitch ⅛″ from the edges.

2 With right sides up, position the trim 2½″ down from the top edge of the exterior back panel, covering the raw ends of the straps and handle. Topstitch ⅛″ from the edges.

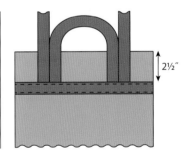

prepare the back lining

1 Fold the slip pocket in half with wrong sides together to measure 12″ × 9″. Press. Topstitch ¼″ from the fold.

2 Aligning the side and bottom raw edges, position the slip pocket on the lining back panel with the fold toward the top. Baste the side and bottom edges of the slip pocket in place with a ¼″ seam allowance. If desired, stitch a vertical line up the center of the slip pocket to divide it into 2 compartments.

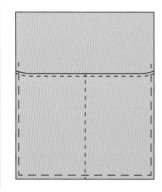

shape the exterior and lining panels

1 On the top edge of the finished exterior and lining panels, measure 1″ in from each side. Draw a diagonal line between each 1″ mark and the bottom corner of each piece. Stitch ⅛″ in from each diagonal line; then cut along the marked line.

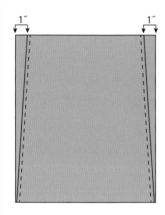

2 Use the 6½″ circle template to round the top corners of the exterior and lining panels. Use the 3½″ circle template to round the bottom corners of each panel. Refer to Shopping Tote, Attach the Cork Base, Step 2 (page 42).

3 Mark the top, bottom, and side centers by folding each panel in half from each direction.

prepare the gusset

1 Fuse the interfacing to the wrong side of the lining zipper-gusset pieces.

2 With right sides together, position a 24″ or longer double-slide zipper along the length of one cork zipper-gusset piece. Close the zipper and put both pulls on one end. Let the zipper pulls and ends of the zipper extend beyond the gusset.

3 With right sides together, layer one lining zipper-gusset piece on top of the zipper and cork zipper gusset. Sew together along the top edge, as shown, with a ¼″ seam allowance.

4 Steam to relax the cork. Press the cork and lining zipper-gusset pieces away from the zipper so they are wrong sides together. Topstitch ¼″ from the seam.

5 Repeat to attach the remaining cork and lining zipper-gusset pieces to the opposite side of the zipper. Make sure to align the side edges.

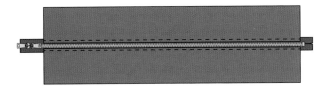

6 Trim the assembled zipper gusset as needed so it measures 5″ wide. Make sure to leave an equal amount of fabric on each side of the zipper. Move the zipper pulls to the center; then trim off the excess zipper tape.

TIP

To trim the cork fabric accurately, take a long quilting ruler and center the zipper coil along the 2½″ line. Use a rotary cutter to trim off the excess. Repeat to trim the excess fabric from the opposite side, making sure the final width of the zipper panel measures 5″ wide.

7 Align one end of the cork bottom gusset with one end of the zipper gusset. Align one end of the lining bottom gusset with the same short end of the zipper gusset. Sew the layers together.

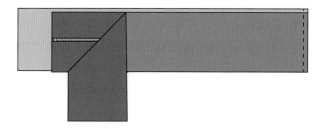

8 Steam to relax the cork. Press the bottom gusset pieces away from the zipper gusset so they are wrong sides together. Topstitch ⅝″ from the seam. Repeat to attach the other ends of the bottom gusset pieces to the other end of the zipper gusset.

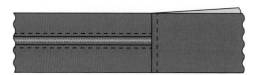

9 Mark the top, bottom, and side centers by folding the assembled gusset in half from each direction.

assemble the backpack

1 With wrong sides together, align all edges of the exterior front panel and the lining front panel. Sew together with a ¼″ seam allowance. Repeat for the exterior back panel and the lining back panel, making sure the straps are out of the way.

2 With the cork fabric right side against the exterior fabric and the zippers at the top, match the center marks on the gusset with the center marks on the exterior front panel. Use sewing clips to hold together the center marks first, then the straight edges, and lastly the curves.

TIP

Use small scissors to clip ⅛″ notches on the edge of the gusset to help ease the cork around the curves.

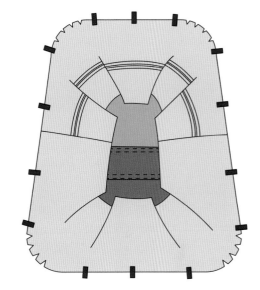

3 Stitch with a ¼″ seam allowance. Stitch only the front to the gusset at this point.

TIP

It's easiest to complete this step by sewing with the exterior panel against the bed of the sewing machine.

4 Refer to How to Make and Attach Binding (page 17) to enclose the seam allowances with bias binding.

5 Repeat the same process to attach the exterior back panel to the other side of the gusset piece. Bind the seam allowance with the remainder of the binding strip.

secure the straps to the backpack

With the right side of each adjustable strap up, thread the unsewn end through the rectangle ring below from the outside towards the inside. Next, thread each end back through the slider buckle from underneath towards the top, over the center bar, and back down towards the bottom. Fold the strap onto itself and topstitch ⅛″ and ¼″ from the end.

REVERSE APPLIQUÉ POUCH

Creating reverse appliqué is easy with cork fabric! There is no need to finish off the raw edges like in traditional reverse appliqué techniques. This simple pouch could also be made without the reverse appliqué for a more beginner-friendly project. Use this pouch as a wristlet or to help organize items in your purse.

Fabric: Surface Natural Cork Fabric by Sallie Tomato. Choose a lining fabric from your stash.

materials

Cork (27″ wide): ¼ yard for pouch, strap connector, and wrist strap

Main fabric: ⅛ yard *or* scraps for appliqué

Lining: ⅓ yard

½″ D-ring

¾″ swivel hook

Small rivet

8″ zipper

Fine-point marker *or* ink pen

Fabric glue *or* temporary spray adhesive

Double-sided basting tape

Precision knife

Zipper foot

cutting

Refer to How to Use the Patterns (page 20) to make templates from the patterns.

Templates: Make templates using the 3½″ circle pattern (page 119) and the Reverse Appliqué Pouch horizontal or vertical pattern (page 121).

Cork

- Cut 1 pouch 9″ × 12″.
- Cut 1 strap connector ½″ × 1½″.
- Cut 2 wrist straps 1½″ × 9″.

Main fabric: Cut 1 appliqué piece 4″ × 8″.

Lining: Cut 1 pouch 8¾″ × 11¾″.

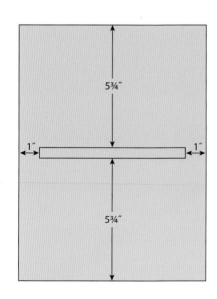

CONSTRUCTION

Seam allowances are ½″ unless otherwise noted.

prepare the exterior

1 Mark a placement box for the zipper on the wrong side of the cork pouch piece. Measure and mark a line 5¾″ in from each 9″ side. Mark a vertical line 1″ in from each 12″ side. This will create a box. Cut on the marked lines.

2 Use the 3½″ circle template to round the corners of the cork pouch piece, as shown in Shopping Tote, Attach the Cork Base, Step 2 (page 42).

reverse appliqué

1 Choose either of the arrow templates/layouts provided. Carefully cut out the inside of the arrow designs using scissors or a precision knife.

2 Center the template on the lower half of the cork pouch piece against the right side. Trace the arrow design onto the pouch using a fine-point marker or ink pen.

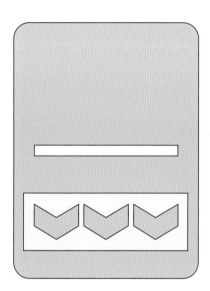

TIP
You can use a permanent-ink marker to trace inside the appliqué template because the lines will be cut in the next step. You can trace on the backside of the cork if you prefer, but the cuts may not be as clean.

3 Cut on the outer edge of the marked lines. Take your time to cut accurately.

TIP
I start by cutting the straight edges of the design with a ruler and a 28 mm rotary cutter. I cut close to the corners but not past them. Then I use a pair of small scissors to clip the corners.

4 Adhere double-sided basting tape to the wrong side of the pouch along the outer edges of the cutout arrow design.

5 With wrong sides up, position the appliqué fabric piece over the cut-out design, covering it completely. Press down to adhere the fabric to the tape. Turn the pouch over to the right side and topstitch ⅛″ from all the raw edges of the design. Do not backstitch. Leave a tail of thread at the ends.

6 Pull the thread tails to the wrong side and tie in a knot to secure. On the wrong side, trim the excess appliqué fabric about ¼″ from the topstitching.

prepare the strap connector and wrist strap

1 Slide the D-ring over the end of the strap connector so the D-ring is in the center and the flat side of the hardware is against the wrong side. Fold the connector in half, matching the short raw edges. Use a sewing clip to hold the edges in place.

2 Slide the swivel hook over the end of one wrist strap piece. With right sides together, align the ends of the wrist strap pieces. Sew the ends with a ¼" seam allowance.

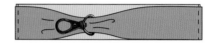

3 Finger-press each seam open. Topstitch ⅛" on each side of the seams.

4 With wrong sides together, fold the strap in half so it now measures ¾" wide. Topstitch ⅛" from the edges. Move the swivel hook out of the way as you sew.

5 Pinch the strap close to the swivel hook. Insert a rivet close to the swivel hook using the manufacturer's instructions, or stitch across the strap close to the hook. Set the strap aside.

prepare the lining

1 Mark a placement box for the zipper on the wrong side of the lining piece. Measure and mark a line 5½" in from each 8¾" side. Mark a vertical line ¾" in from each 11¾" side. This will create a box. Cut on the marked lines.

2 Use the 3½" circle template to round each of the 4 corners of the lining piece, as shown in Shopping Tote, Attach the Cork Base, Step 2 (page 42).

assemble the pouch

1 With wrong sides together, center the lining over the cork pouch piece. Use fabric glue or temporary spray adhesive to hold the layers together.

2 Adhere double-sided basting tape to the right side of the zipper tape.

3 With right sides up, center the zipper inside the placement box. Topstitch ⅛" from the edges of the placement box.

4 Fold the pouch in half with the zipper along the top edge. Tuck the raw end of the strap connector between one side of the lining and cork, ½" down from the top edge. Use sewing clips to hold the layers together. Topstitch ⅛" and ⅜" from the side and bottom edges.

5 Clip the swivel hook to the D-ring on the pouch.

SKILL LEVEL: BEGINNER

Finished tote:
15″ wide × 12″ high × 5½″ deep

APPLIQUÉ TOTE

Use cork fabric for simple and stunning appliqué. You can leave the edges of cork raw, which makes this a great project for beginners. The texture of cork fabric makes each design unique. Use this tote for storage, for trips to the market, or as a beach bag. Making this bag will teach you the basics of appliqué as well as how to add shape to a simple bag.

Fabrics: Surface Natural Cork Fabric by Sallie Tomato for appliqué, top panel, and handles; Infused Hydrangea Denim by Art Gallery Fabrics for bag exterior. Choose a lining fabric from your stash.

materials

Cork (27″ wide): ⅓ yard for appliqué, handles, and top panel

Main fabric: ⅔ yard for exterior panels

Lining: 1 yard

Fusible fleece: ¼ yard for top panel

Foam stabilizer (20″ wide): 1⅓ yards for main panel

Tailor's chalk *or* **air-erasable marker**

Fabric glue *or* **temporary spray adhesive**

Appliqué presser foot (*optional*)

cutting

Refer to How to Use the Patterns (page 20) to make templates from the patterns.

Templates: Make templates using the Appliqué Tote large petal, small petal, and circle patterns (page 121).

Cork

- Cut 4 large petals, 12 small petals, and 1 circle using the templates.
- Cut 1 piece 2″ × width of fabric for the handles.
- Cut 2 pieces 2½″ × 22″ for the top panels.

Main fabric: Cut 2 pieces 22″ × 15″ for the exterior panels.

Lining

- Cut 2 pieces 22″ × 16½″ for the lining.
- Cut 1 piece 10″ × 10″ for the patch pocket.

Fusible fleece: Cut 2 pieces 2½″ × 22″ for the top panels.

Foam stabilizer: Cut 2 pieces 22″ × 15″ for the exterior panels.

CONSTRUCTION

Seam allowances are ½″ unless otherwise noted.

prepare the exterior

1 With wrong sides together, align the edges of each exterior panel with one piece of foam stabilizer. Sew the edges together with an ⅛″ seam allowance.

TIP

I prefer using sew-in foam stabilizer rather than fusible foam stabilizer because fusible foam usually wrinkles after turning the bag right side out. Instead, spray the back of your fabric with temporary spray adhesive to hold the sew-in stabilizer in place.

2 On the right side of each main panel, measure and mark 3½″ in from the sides and the bottom. Stitch on the marked lines to add shape to the tote.

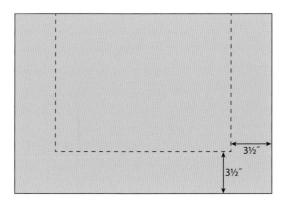

APPLIQUÉ

1 Measure and mark a vertical line 11″ from the sides and a horizontal line 6″ from the top on the right side of one exterior panel. Mark ¼″ on each side of both lines.

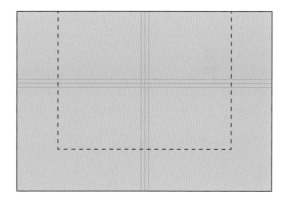

2 Position each of the 4 large petals as shown. Try your best to align one corner of each petal with the marked lines of a 90° angle. Apply fabric glue or temporary adhesive to the wrong side of each petal to hold it in place.

3 Position the small petals with the tips 1¼″ from the nearest marked line and with the sides ¼″ from the sides of the large petals. Adhere in place.

4 Position the remaining petals, spaced ¼″ from the other petals. Layer the circle appliqué over the center of the design. Adhere in place.

5 Using your desired stitch and an appliqué presser foot, sew the petals to the exterior panels.

TIP

I used a straight stitch, sewing ⅛″ from the raw edge. You could also try a zigzag stitch, satin stitch, or decorative stitch. Test your stitch first on a scrap to make sure it isn't too dense. Too many holes in your cork may cause it to tear.

MAKE THE HANDLES AND ATTACH THEM TO THE TOP PANELS

1 Apply fabric glue or adhesive spray to the wrong side of the cork handle piece on the long edges. Fold each long side to the center and press down to adhere it in place. Stitch along each long side, ⅛″ from the center.

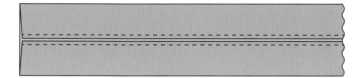

2 Cut the handle in half, making 2 handles. Set the handles aside.

3 Fuse the fusible fleece to the wrong side of each top panel.

TIP

The fusible fleece ensures that the cork top panels are similar in thickness to the exterior front and back panels because they have stabilizer foam attached. It is easier to sew similar-weight fabrics together and add structure to your bag.

4 On the right side of each top panel, measure and mark vertical lines 7¾″ in from each end. On each handle, measure and mark 1½″ from the ends.

5 With right sides up and raw edges together, position each handle inside the marked vertical lines on each top panel. Topstitch the ends of handles ⅛″ from the edge up to the 1½″ line, across the line, and back down the other side.

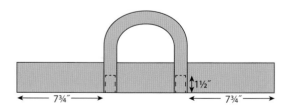

attach the top panels

1 With right sides together, align the bottom edge of a top panel with the top edge of an exterior panel and sew together. Press the seam towards the exterior panel so the cork is flat. Topstitch ¼″ from the seam.

2 Repeat to join the remaining top panel and exterior panel.

make the lining patch pocket

1 Fold the patch pocket in half with right sides together so the pocket measures 10″ × 5″. Align the side and bottom edges and stitch, leaving a 3″ opening on the bottom edge.

2 Trim the corners and side seam allowances to ¼″.

3 Turn the patch pocket right side out. Tuck the raw edges of the opening to the wrong side so the folds are even with the bottom edge. Press. Topstitch ⅛″ and ¼″ from the top edge.

4 With the right sides up, center the pocket 4″ down from the top edge of one lining piece. Topstitch the side and bottom edges of the pocket ⅛″ and ¼″ from the edge. This will close the opening in the bottom of the pocket. If desired, stitch a vertical line through the center of the pocket to divide it into 2 compartments.

assemble the bag

1 Place both exterior pieces right sides together, aligning all edges. Sew together along the side and bottom edges with a ½″ seam allowance.

2 Cut a 3″ square out of each bottom corner.

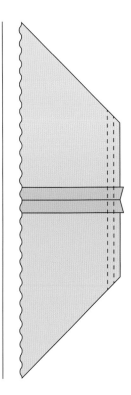

3 Separate the layers of each bottom corner. With right sides together, match the bottom seam and the adjacent side seam to create boxed corners. Sew together with a ½″ seam, making sure to backstitch at each end. Stitch a second seam ¼″ away from the first for reinforcement. Trim off the corners. Leave the exterior wrong side out.

4 Repeat for the lining pieces, but this time leave a 6″ opening in the bottom seam for turning. Turn the lining right side out.

TIP
To help your lining fit better inside your bag, start with a ½″ seam allowance at the top and gradually increase the seam allowance to ¾″ as you reach the bottom edge. Sew across the bottom with a ¾″ seam allowance, and gradually decrease your seam back to ½″ as you reach the top edge of the opposite side. Trim the seam allowance to ¼″.

ATTACH THE LINING AND EXTERIOR

1 With right sides together, put the lining inside the exterior, aligning the top edges and side seams. Sew the top edges together, making sure the handles are tucked inside the bag.

2 Turn the bag right side out by pushing the exterior and lining through the opening in the bottom of the lining.

3 Hand sew or topstitch the opening in the lining closed with an ⅛″ seam allowance, tucking in the raw edges.

4 Push the lining down into the exterior and arrange in place. Topstitch ¼″ from the top edges.

TIP
Use your fingers to roll the top seam to make sure the top edges are aligned and flat before top-stitching.

home decor

Since cork fabric is a very durable, low-maintenance material, it is perfect for home decor items. I've designed the following projects so you can incorporate cork fabric in every room of your house!

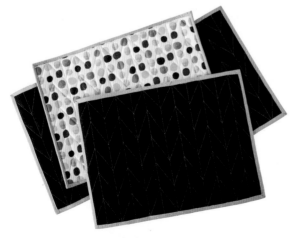

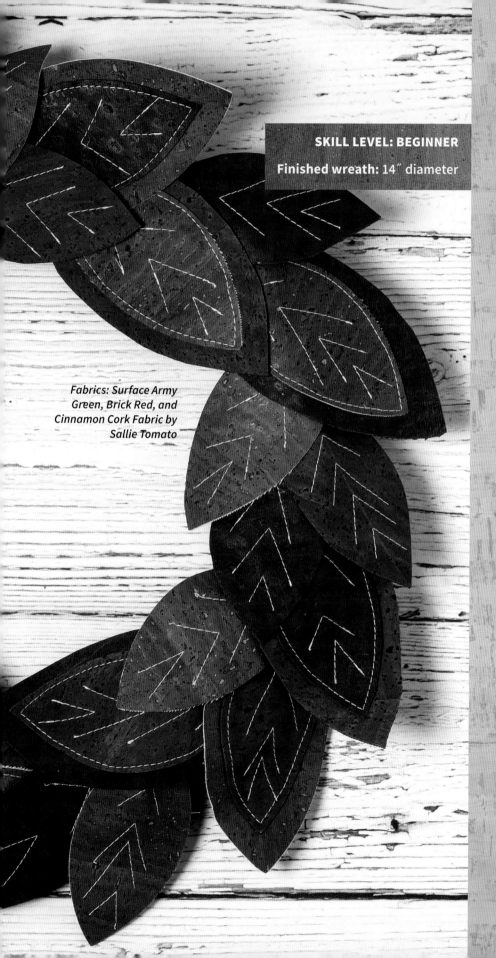

Fabrics: Surface Army Green, Brick Red, and Cinnamon Cork Fabric by Sallie Tomato

WREATH

Brighten up your home or a special event with a handmade wreath made from cork fabric! This is a great project for using up scraps, and practicing stitching on cork and layering a variety of cork pieces. By using different color combinations, you can create a cork wreath for every occasion and season!

materials

Choose 3 different colors of cork fabric (A, B, and C) for the leaves.

Cork A, B, and C (each 27″ wide): ¼ yard *each*

Quilting thread: 12, 30, 40, *or* 50 weight

Twig wreath: 12″ diameter

Hot glue gun and glue

> **TIP**
>
> If you can't find a twig wreath or don't like using hot glue, you can use a 12″ foam wreath and floral pins.

cutting

Refer to How to Use the Patterns (page 20) to make templates using the patterns.

Templates: Make templates using the Wreath large and small leaf patterns (page 121).

Cork A, B, and C: From each cork fabric, cut 4 large leaves and 9 small leaves using the templates.

CONSTRUCTION

layer and embellish the leaves

1 Arrange the small leaves on top of the large leaves, making sure the cork B and C leaves are on top of the A leaves, the cork A and C leaves are on top of the B leaves, and the cork A and B leaves are on top of the C leaves. Hot glue or stitch the small leaves in place. You can refer to the illustration and photograph for stitching ideas or stitch as you wish.

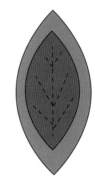

> **TIP**
>
> If you choose to stitch the small leaves in place, you can simply sew ⅛″ around the edge with a straight stitch or decorative stitch. Otherwise, you can stitch vein lines across the leaf for more embellishment.

2 If desired, you can repeat the same stitch pattern you used on the large, layered leaves to embellish the remaining small leaves.

assemble the wreath

1 On your worktable, arrange the leaves randomly in a circle to get an idea of how you want to place them.

TIP
First, I arranged matching layered large leaves across from each other. Then I filled in the gaps with the small leaves. This way, the cork colors were evenly spaced around the wreath.

2 Secure the leaves to the twig wreath by applying hot glue to the wrong side of a leaf and holding it in place on the wreath while the glue dries.

TIP
It is fun to come up with thematic and seasonal wreaths. Make it patriotic with red, white, and denim-blue cork fabric to make a festive Fourth of July wreath! Or use light-pink, white, and mint-green cork fabric to make a pastel cork wreath for a newborn's room or as a last-minute baby shower gift!

REVERSIBLE PLACE MAT SET

This project is meant to get you comfortable with quilting cork fabric on your sewing machine! Easily customize these place mats with your desired quilting design. The simplicity of these place mats allows for a professional finished project. And they are so easy to clean—simply wipe with a warm, soapy cloth or pop in the washing machine!

SKILL LEVEL: BEGINNER

Finished place mat: 18″ × 13″

Fabrics: Surface Denim Blue Cork Fabric by Sallie Tomato for place mat fronts; Painted Dots (Blue) by Alexia Abegg for Cotton + Steel for place mat backs

materials

Material requirements are for 1 set of 4 place mats. Batting can be substituted for the sew-in foam if desired.

Cork (27″ wide): 1 yard for place mat fronts

Cotton A: 1 yard for place mat backs

Cotton B: ⅝ yard for binding

Foam (60″ wide): ½ yard

Quilting thread: 12, 30, 40, *or* 50 weight

Temporary spray adhesive

cutting

Cork: Cut 2 strips 18″ × width of fabric; subcut a total of 4 pieces 18″ × 13″ for the place mat fronts.

Cotton A: Cut 2 strips 15″ × width of fabric; subcut a total of 4 pieces 20″ × 15″ for the place mat backs.

Cotton B: Cut 7 strips 2½″ × width of fabric for the binding.

Foam: Cut 4 pieces 18″ × 13″.

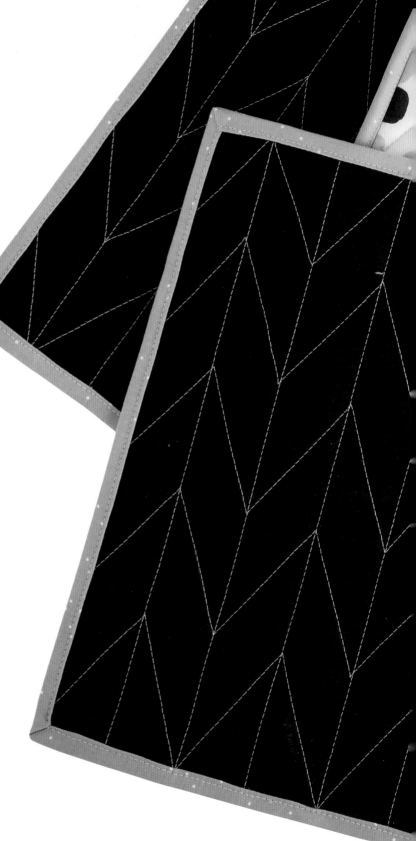

CONSTRUCTION

quilt

1 Place one place mat back on a clean, flat surface with the wrong side up.

2 Center one piece of foam on top of the place mat back. There should be about 1″ of the place mat back extending beyond all 4 sides.

3 Layer one place mat front on top of the foam with the right side up, aligning the edges.

TIP

Try using a temporary spray adhesive to hold the layers together rather than pins or sewing clips. Pins can damage your cork fabric by leaving a permanent hole. Simply spray the wrong side of each layer; then press down and smooth out the wrinkles to temporarily adhere the pieces together.

4 Measure and mark 11 vertical lines spaced 1½″ apart.

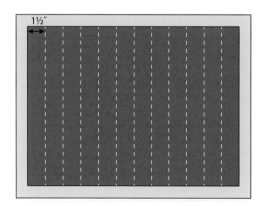

5 Mark horizontal lines ¼″ from the top and bottom edges. Measure and mark 4 horizontal lines spaced 2½″ apart between the ¼″ lines.

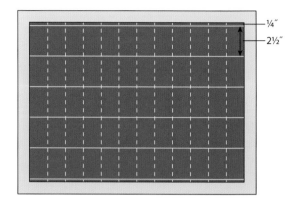

6 Mark diagonal lines between the intersections. Quilt only the vertical and diagonal lines.

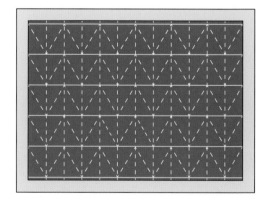

7 Repeat to make a set of 4 place mats.

TIP

Quilt your place mats as desired. Try quilting an allover design, vertical rows with a straight stitch, or decorative stitches! Try using a heavier-weight quilting thread, such as Superior's Sew Sassy, for a more defined stitch. However, your favorite weight of quilting thread will work equally well for this project.

finish

1 Trim away the excess fabric so it is even with the edges of the cork.

2 Follow How to Make and Attach Binding (page 17), or bind the place mats as desired.

TIP

Since these place mats are reversible, use a holiday fabric for the back to easily switch from your everyday look to festive in no time! Or piece scraps or leftover quilt blocks to make the reverse side of these cork place mats look quilty!

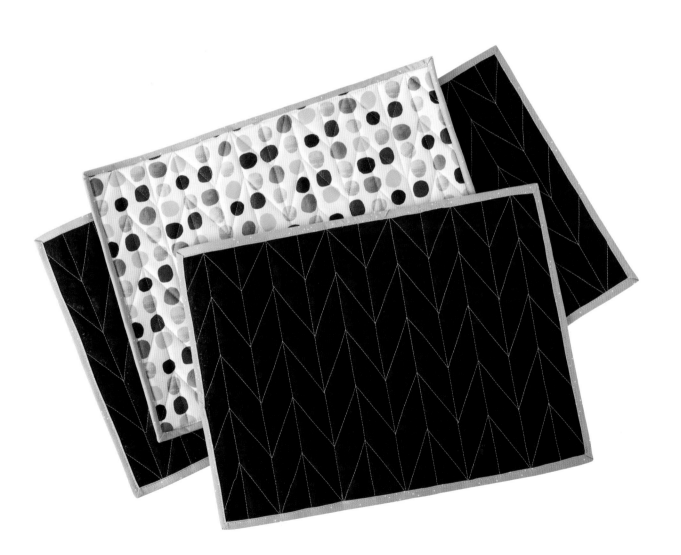

WOVEN STORAGE BASKET

I love to organize my home and sewing space, so I've designed this stylish, sturdy storage basket made from cork fabric to help you organize, too! This basket is simple to sew and uses a weaving technique to add support. Use your favorite quilt cotton to make a basket liner for easy cleaning and visual appeal.

Fabrics: Surface Cinnamon Cork Fabric by Sallie Tomato for basket; Rosa (Natural) by Rifle Paper Co. for Cotton + Steel for lining

materials

Cork (27″ wide): 27″ for basket exterior and side strips

Lining: ⅝ yard

Tailor's chalk *or* **air-erasable marker**

Hot glue gun and glue

cutting

Cork

- Cut 1 strip 18″ × width of fabric; subcut 2 pieces 13″ × 18″ for the basket exterior.
- Cut 8 strips 1⅛″ × width of fabric for the side strips.

Lining: Cut 2 pieces 13″ × 18″.

CONSTRUCTION

Seam allowances are ½″ unless otherwise noted.

prepare the exterior

1 On the wrong side of each basket exterior, measure and mark horizontal lines 4″ from the top and bottom edges. Between the lines, mark vertical lines 1″ apart.

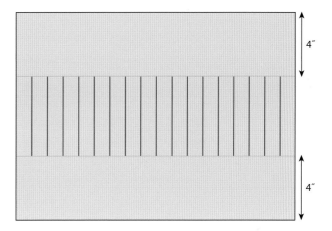

2 Cut on the marked vertical lines.

3 With right sides together, align the edges of the exterior pieces. Sew together on the side and bottom edges.

4 Cut a 3½″ square from the bottom corners.

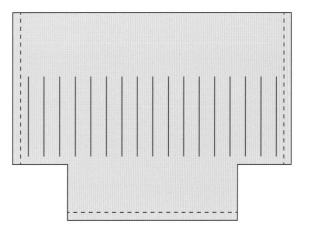

5 Finger-press the side seam allowances open. If your machine allows, topstitch each side of the seams with a ¼″ seam allowance.

6 Separate the layers of each bottom corner. With right sides together, match the bottom seam and the adjacent side seam to create boxed corners. Sew together with a ½″ seam allowance, making sure to backstitch at each end. Stitch a second seam, ¼″ away from the first, for reinforcement. Trim off the corners. Turn the basket right side out.

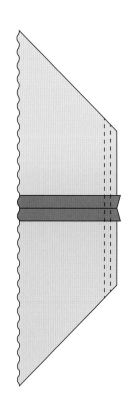

7 Fold the top edge of the basket 2″ to the wrong side. Topstitch along the cut edge and again ⅛″ down from the top fold.

8 Use hot glue to join 2 strips 1⅛″ × width of fabric by overlapping a narrow end of the 2 strips by ½″. Trim the strip to 35″ long. Repeat to make a total of 4 strips.

9 With right sides out, start by weaving one strip behind one vertical strip. Then weave it in front of the next vertical strip. Continue weaving until you reach the beginning. Hot glue the raw ends of the strip together, overlapping ¼″. Push the strip tight against the bottom of the cut opening.

10 Continue weaving strips until you reach the top. Set the basket aside.

make and insert the lining

1 With right sides together, align all edges of the lining pieces. Sew together on the side and bottom edges.

2 Cut a 3½" square from the bottom corners.

3 Create boxed corners as described in Step 6 (previous page). Leave the lining wrong side out.

4 Press the top edge of the lining ¼" to the wrong side and then ¼" to the wrong side again. Top-stitch ⅛" from the folded edge.

5 With wrong sides together, insert the lining into the basket. Fold the top edge of the lining over the top edge of the basket. Now your basket is ready to use!

CUSTOM PENNANT BANNER

SKILL LEVEL: BEGINNER

Finished pennant: 10″ × 16″

Make a custom pennant banner to display your favorite short phrase! Use cork fabric to make the lettering and use cotton or canvas for the background.

Fabrics: Surface Black, White, and Yellow Cork Fabric by Sallie Tomato for letters; Maker collection from Art Gallery Fabrics for pennants

AKE
TUFF

QUILT
TALK

materials

Material requirements are for 1 pennant.
The photograph shows 3 pennants.

Cork (27″ wide): ⅛ yard for letters

Pennant fabric: ½ yard

Lightweight woven fusible interfacing (20″ wide): ⅔ yard for pennant

Ribbon or twine: 20″ length

Wooden dowel (½″ diameter): 14″ long

Tailor's chalk *or* **air-erasable marker**

Fabric glue *or* **temporary spray adhesive**

Appliqué presser foot

> **TIP**
>
> Make a pennant for the kitchen by using novelty print fabrics with clever kitchen phrases or decorate a child's room with multiple pennants in colorful fabrics, covered with inspirational phrases!

cutting

Refer to How to Use the Patterns (page 20) to make templates from the patterns.

Templates: Make templates using the alphabet patterns (pages 122 and 123).

Cork: Cut the desired letters using the templates.

> **TIP**
>
> Keep in mind that you can only fit 5 letters across in each of the 2 sections. Thus, the maximum number of letters you can use is 10.

Pennant fabric: Cut 2 pennant pieces 11″ × 17″.

Lightweight woven fusible interfacing: Cut 2 pennant pieces 11″ × 17″.

CONSTRUCTION

Seam allowances are ½″ unless otherwise noted.

attach the appliqués

1 Fuse one piece of lightweight woven fusible interfacing to the wrong side of each pennant piece.

2 On the right side of one pennant piece, mark a vertical line 1″ in from the sides. Measure and mark 4 horizontal lines to divide the pennant into 3 sections 3″ and 1 section 1″, as shown.

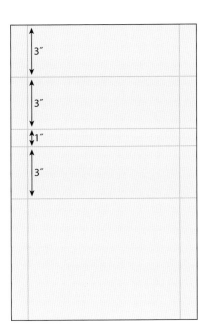

3 Equally space your letters on the right side of the fabric, in the lower 2 sections 3″, as shown. Apply fabric glue or temporary spray adhesive to the wrong side of each letter to hold it in place.

4 Use your desired stitch and an appliqué presser foot to sew each of the letters to the pennant piece. I recommend a straight stitch, sewing ⅛″ from the raw edge, or a long zigzag stitch. Remove the marked lines.

assemble the pennant

1 On the bottom edge of each pennant piece, mark the center and 4″ up from the bottom on each side. Draw a diagonal line between the center and each 4″ mark. Cut along the diagonal lines to create an angled bottom edge.

2 With right sides together, align all edges of the 2 pennant pieces. Sew the side and bottom edges, leaving the top edge open for turning. Use scissors to diagonally trim away the seam allowance at the corners. Turn the pennant right side out through the top.

3 Press. Topstitch ¼″ from the side and bottom edges.

4 Fold the top edge ½″ to the back side. Topstitch ⅛″ from the fold.

5 Fold the top edge 1¼″ to the back side so it aligns with the previously marked topmost horizontal line. Topstitch ¼″ from that fold to create a casing for the wooden dowel.

6 Insert the wooden dowel into the casing. Tie the opposite ends of the ribbon to the ends the dowel.

TIP
Simply hang your completed pennant from a doorknob, or hang the pennant by a nail or sticky hook on wall. Place multiple pennant banners in a row for fun, inspirational wall art!

Fabrics: Cork Fabric by Sallie Tomato for appliqué. Any quilt-weight cotton or linen for background and backing.

SKILL LEVEL: BEGINNER

Finished wallhanging: 8″ × 18″

MOD TREE WALLHANGING

It's super easy to make wall art with cork fabric appliqué. Use scraps or a minimal amount of cork to create this Mod Tree Wallhanging.

materials

Material requirements are for 1 wallhanging.

Cork A (27″ wide): ⅛ yard for large mod leaf

Cork B (27″ wide): 4″ for small mod leaf

Cork C (27″ wide): 1″ for trunk and branches

Main fabric: ½ yard for background

Backing: ⅓ yard

Lightweight woven fusible interfacing: ¼ yard for background

Batting: ⅓ yard

Fabric glue *or* **temporary spray adhesive**

Appliqué presser foot

cutting

Refer to How to Use the Patterns (page 20) to make templates from the patterns.

Templates: Make templates using the Mod Tree Wallhanging large and small leaf patterns (pages 124 and 125).

Cork A: Cut 1 large mod leaf using the template.

Cork B: Cut 1 small mod leaf using the template.

Cork C

- Cut 1 trunk 1″ × 12″.
- Cut 2 A branches ½″ × 2″.
- Cut 2 B branches ¼″ × 1½″.
- Cut 1 C branch ¼″ × 1″.

Main fabric

- Cut 1 background 8″ × 18″.
- Cut 2 strips 2″ × width of fabric for the binding.

Backing: Cut 1 backing 10″ × 20″.

Lightweight woven fusible interfacing: Cut 1 background 8″ × 18″.

Batting: Cut 1 piece 10″ × 20″.

CONSTRUCTION

Seam allowances are ¼″ unless otherwise noted.

attach the appliqué

1 Fuse the lightweight woven fusible interfacing to the wrong side of the background fabric.

2 With the right side up, position the large mod leaf 4½″ up from the bottom edge of the background. Apply fabric glue or temporary spray adhesive to the wrong side of the leaf to hold it in place.

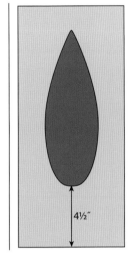

4½″

3 With the right side up, position the small mod leaf 5½˝ up from the bottom edge of the background. Adhere it in place.

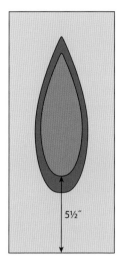

4 Use your desired stitch and appliqué presser foot to sew each of the leaves to the background. I recommend a straight stitch, sewing ⅛˝ from the raw edges.

5 Mark the center on the top edge of the trunk and branch pieces. On each piece, draw a diagonal line between the top center and each bottom corner. Cut along the diagonal lines to angle the side edges of each piece.

6 With right sides up, center the trunk on the bottom edge of the background. Position the branches as shown, tucking the bottom edge of each branch under the trunk. Adhere in place.

7 Sew the trunk and branch pieces in place ⅛˝ from the raw edges.

quilt

1 Lay the backing on a clean, flat surface with the wrong side up.

2 Center the batting on top of the backing, aligning all edges.

3 With right sides up, center the background on top of the batting.

TIP
Try using a temporary spray adhesive to hold the layers together. Simply spray the wrong side of each layer, press down, and smooth out the wrinkles to temporarily adhere the pieces together.

4 Quilt your wallhanging as desired. I recommend quilting only the background around the appliqué to make the cork fabric pop!

finish

1 Trim the excess fabric even with the edges of the background.

2 Follow How to Make and Attach Binding (page 17) or bind as desired.

accessories

I hope you've been saving your scraps! These projects are great for using your treasured bits and pieces of cork.

SKILL LEVEL: BEGINNER

Finished mini tassel: ½″ × 2″

Finished standard tassel: 1″ × 4″

TASSEL TUTORIAL

Save all your cork fabric scraps and use them to make tassels to accessorize your projects. Instructions are provided so you can make two different tassel sizes and attach them in two different ways. One technique (version A) is for attaching tassels with a swivel clip (or O-ring, D-ring, or any such hardware) and the other technique (version B) uses a long fabric or cork connector to hang a tassel from the handle of any bag.

Fabrics: Cork Fabric by Sallie Tomato

materials

Try using up some of your scraps!

Cork (27″ wide): ⅛ yard for tassel and connector

½″ D-ring, O-ring, or swivel clip for version A

Hot glue gun and glue

mini tassel cutting

Cork

- Cut 1 tassel 2″ × 2″.
- Cut 1 version A tassel connector ¼″ × 1½″.
- Cut 1 version B tassel connector ¼″ × 14″.

standard tassel cutting

Cork

- Cut 1 tassel 4″ × 4″.
- Cut 1 version A tassel connector ½″ × 1½″.
- Cut 1 version B tassel connector ½″ × 14″.

Tassel attached with O-ring

Tassel attached with fabric connector

CONSTRUCTION

1 On the wrong side of the tassel piece, mark a horizontal line ½″ down from the top edge. Using a rotary cutter or scissors, cut the tassel fringe from the bottom up to the marked line, about ¼″ apart across the entire width.

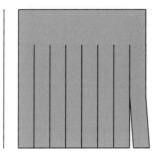

2 For both versions A and B, apply hot glue to one end of the tassel connector. Position the connector on the left edge of the tassel against the ½″ mark.

TIP
First topstitch the connector ⅛″ from the long edges for an extra touch!

3 If you're making version A, slide the swivel clip over the end of the connector so the swivel clip is in the center and the flat side of the hardware is against the wrong side.

4 Fold the connector in half, matching the short raw edges. Glue in place.

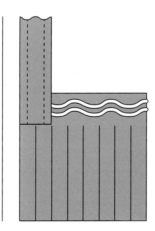

5 Wrap and glue the tassel to itself along the top edge; wrap as tight as possible.

6 If you're making version A, clip the swivel clip to your project. If you're making version B, bring the connector around a handle. Then thread the tassel through the folded end of the tassel connector and pull tight to secure it on the handle.

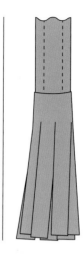

MINIMALIST CORK NECKLACE

Cork is a great material to use for jewelry because it looks and feels like quality leather. Use cork for a simple, natural look. This necklace is perfect for a minimalist or bohemian style!

SKILL LEVEL: BEGINNER

Finished necklace:
2½″ × 5″ without chain
2½″ × 41″ with chain

Fabric: Cork Fabric by Sallie Tomato

materials

A perfect project for using your cork scraps!

Cork (27″ wide): 3″ for arrows

Jump rings (½″ diameter): 6

Necklace chain: 36″ long

Fabric glue *or* **temporary spray adhesive**

Rotary punch *or* **awl**

Flat-nose pliers

cutting

Refer to How to Use the Patterns (page 20) to make templates from the patterns.

Templates

• Make a template using the Minimalist Cork Necklace arrow pattern (page 124).

Cork

• Cut 1 backing 3″ × 6″.

• Cut 3 arrows using the template.

CONSTRUCTION

1 With wrong sides together, equally space the 3 arrows on the backing piece. Use fabric glue or temporary spray adhesive to hold the arrows in place.

2 Topstitch the arrows to the backing ⅛″ from the edges.

3 Cut out the arrows along the raw edges.

4 Use a rotary punch or awl to punch a ⅛″-diameter hole just inside the stitching on all 4 outer corners of 2 arrows and on the 2 top corners of the remaining arrow.

5 Connect the arrows by inserting jump rings through the holes. Connect the assembled arrows to the ends of the necklace chain by inserting jump rings through the holes and chain.

TIP

To open a jump ring, do not pull it apart. This will distort and weaken the ring. Instead use flat nose pliers to spread each side of the ring apart in opposite directions.

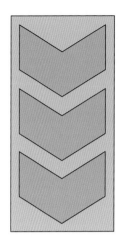

EASY BOX POUCH

A box pouch made from cork fabric makes an easy gift for guys and gals. Stuff it with shaving supplies, makeup, sewing notions, small toys, and other items you want to keep organized. This is a great beginner project because there is no lining.

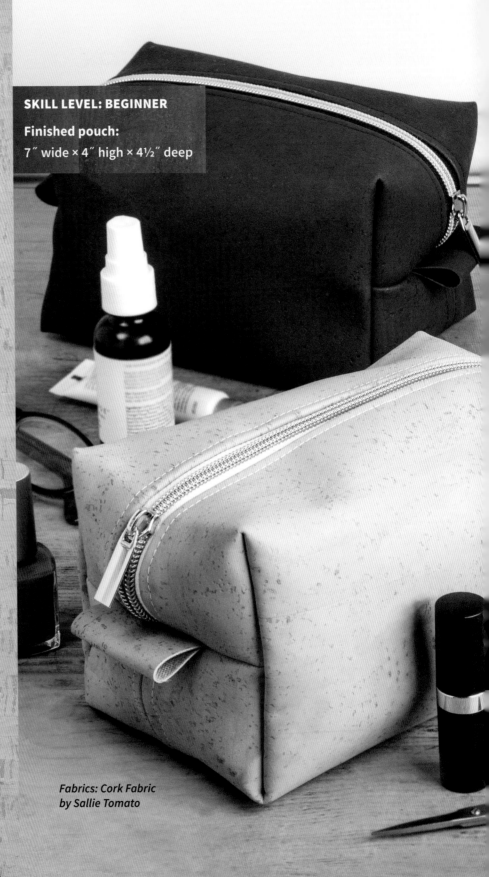

SKILL LEVEL: BEGINNER

Finished pouch:
7″ wide × 4″ high × 4½″ deep

Fabrics: Cork Fabric by Sallie Tomato

materials

Material requirements are for 1 Easy Box Pouch.

Cork (27″ wide): ¼ yard for pouch and loops

15″ zipper or longer

Zipper presser foot

cutting

Cork

- Cut 2 pouch pieces 9″ × 12″.
- Cut 2 loop pieces 2″ × 3″.

CONSTRUCTION

Seam allowances are ½″ unless otherwise noted.

attach the zipper

1 Center a 15″ or longer zipper along a 12″ side of one pouch piece, right sides and top edges together. Using a zipper foot, sew the zipper to the pouch with a ⅜″ seam allowance.

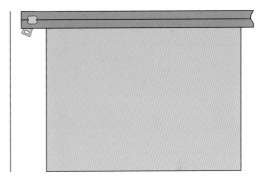

TIP

The zipper is longer so you don't have to worry about the zipper pull getting in the way of the needle or the presser foot.

2 Fold the pouch piece away from the zipper. Topstitch ¼″ from the seam.

3 Repeat to attach and topstitch the opposite side of the zipper to the other pouch piece. Move the zipper pull to the center of the pouch. Trim the excess zipper even with the sides of the pouch.

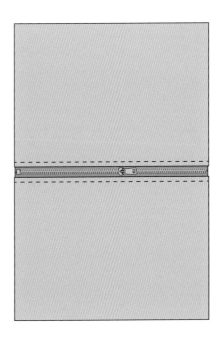

TIP

Stitch across the ends of the zipper to prevent the zipper pull from coming off after trimming.

4 With wrong sides together, fold each of the
loop pieces in half so
they measure 2″ × 1½″.
Stitch the bottom
edges together with a
¼″ seam allowance.

5 With right sides together, center one loop on the
ends of the zipper, aligning the raw edges. Baste
the edges together.

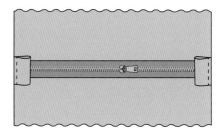

assemble the pouch

1 With right sides together, align the sides and bottom edges of the pouch pieces. Sew the bottom edges
together with a ½″ seam allowance. If your machine allows, topstitch ¼″ from each side of the seam.

TIP
Topstitching the bottom seam is easier if you unzip the zipper.

2 With right sides together, center the zipper over
the bottom seam. Sew the side edges together.

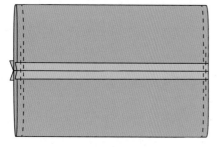

3 Cut a rectangle out of each corner of the pouch,
1½″ from the fold and 2″ from the raw edges.

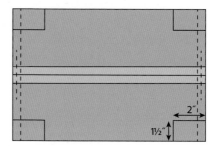

4 Separate the layers of each corner. With right sides together, match the side seam and the adjacent side fold to create boxed corners. Sew together with a ½″ seam, making sure to backstitch at each end. Stitch a second seam, ¼″ away from the first, for reinforcement. Turn the box pouch right side out.

FASHION BELT

Add texture to any outfit with this cork fashion belt! This belt is made according to your measurements, so it will fit you perfectly.

Fabric: Surface Natural Cork Fabric by Sallie Tomato

materials

Cork (27″ wide): ⅓ yard for belt and leaves

Quilting thread: 12, 30, 40, *or* 50 weight

Line 20 snap sets: 2

Fabric glue

Sewing clips

cutting

Refer to How to Use the Patterns (page 20) to make templates from the patterns.

Templates: Make templates from the Fashion Belt large, medium, and small leaf patterns (page 125) and the Fashion Belt circle pattern (page 124).

Cork

• Cut enough 2½″-wide strips to equal the measurement of your natural waist, plus 5″ and enough extra length to join the strips. Add 2½″ for each seam in the strip.

• Cut 6 large leaves, 6 medium leaves, 6 small leaves, and 1 circle using the templates.

CONSTRUCTION

layer the leaves

1 With right sides up, layer the leaves in order as shown. Match the lower points to create a cluster. Use fabric glue to hold the leaves in place.

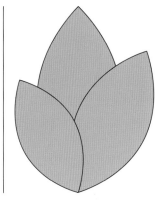

TIP

Alternate the placement of the small and medium leaves for a more natural look.

2 Repeat the same process to make a total of 6 leaf clusters.

assemble the belt

1 Join the belt pieces by placing the ends right sides together, perpendicular to each other. Sew at a 45° angle from edge to edge. Trim the excess seam allowance to ¼″ wide. Press the seam open. Topstitch each side of the seam with an ⅛″ seam allowance.

2 Double-check that the length of your belt is the amount you need. Add another strip or trim the length as necessary.

3 Fold the assembled belt in half lengthwise with wrong sides together. Topstitch ⅛″ from the edges.

4 Fold the belt in half to find the center front. Arrange the leaf clusters from the center outward, with 3 clusters on each side of the center. Use fabric glue or sewing clips to hold the clusters in place. Adhere the circle to the center.

5 Secure the leaf clusters to the belt by sewing through the center length of the belt with a straight stitch.

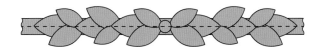

6 Insert opposite halves of each snap, centered ½″ and 2″ in from each end of the belt. Now your belt is ready to wear!

Fabrics: Cork Fabric by Sallie Tomato

JEAN JACKET MAKEOVER

Embellish the back (or front) of any jean jacket with a garden of cork flowers. This project can easily be made from scraps of cork, or you can make two flowers out of a 2˝ strip of cork fabric.

materials

Cork (27″ wide): Scraps *or a* variety of 2″-long strips (Each 2″ strip makes 2 flowers.)

Jean jacket

Hot glue gun and glue

Assortment of beads (¼″–⅜″ diameter; *optional*)

cutting

Refer to How to Use the Patterns (page 20) to make templates from the patterns.

Templates: Make templates using the Jean Jacket Makeover large and small petal patterns (page 124).

Cork

• For each small flower, cut 5 small petals using the template.

• For each layered flower, cut 5 large petals and 5 small petals using the templates.

CONSTRUCTION

assemble the flowers

1 Arrange each of the large petals as shown, overlapping one another without a gap in the center. Apply hot glue to the wrong side of each petal at each overlap to hold the petals in place.

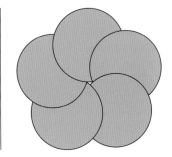

2 Repeat the same process with the small petals, layering the petal clusters as shown. With right sides up, apply a generous amount of hot glue to the back and center of the petal clusters. Press down on the center to adhere the petals in place.

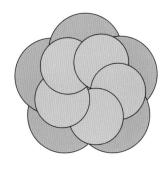

3 If desired, hot glue a bead in the center of each flower.

attach the flowers to the jacket

Arrange the assembled flowers on the back of the jean jacket as desired. Topstitch ⅛″ from the outer edge of each flower, or hot glue the wrong side of each flower to the jacket.

patterns

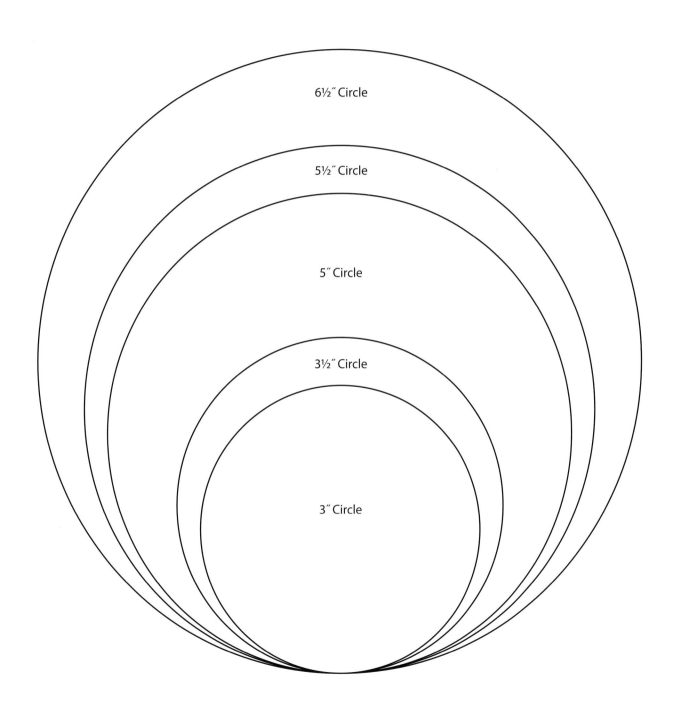

6½˝ Circle

5½˝ Circle

5˝ Circle

3½˝ Circle

3˝ Circle

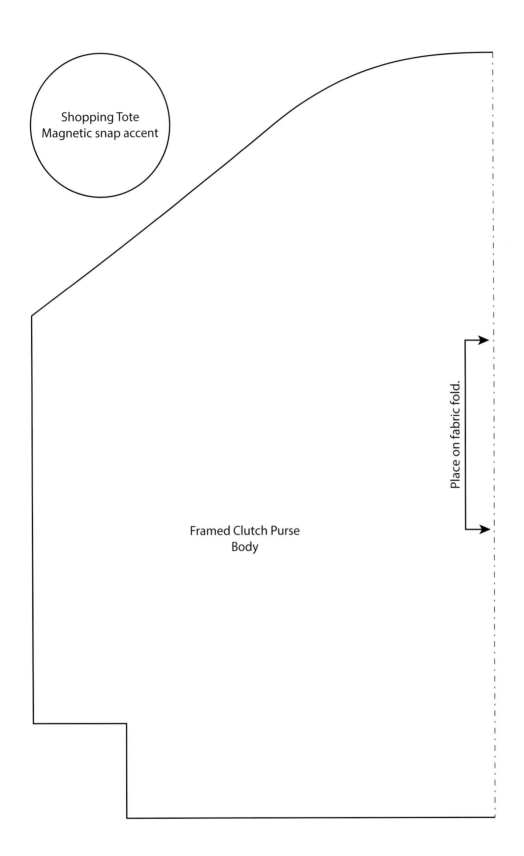

Shopping Tote
Magnetic snap accent

Framed Clutch Purse
Body

Place on fabric fold.

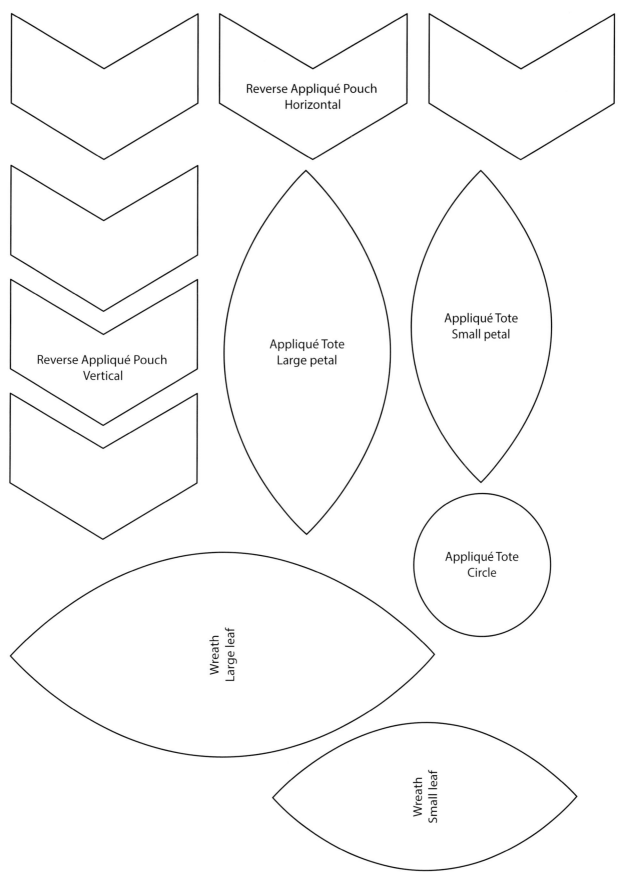

Reverse Appliqué Pouch
Horizontal

Reverse Appliqué Pouch
Vertical

Appliqué Tote
Large petal

Appliqué Tote
Small petal

Appliqué Tote
Circle

Wreath
Large leaf

Wreath
Small leaf

ABCDE
FGHIJ
KLMN

OPQR
STUV
WXYZ

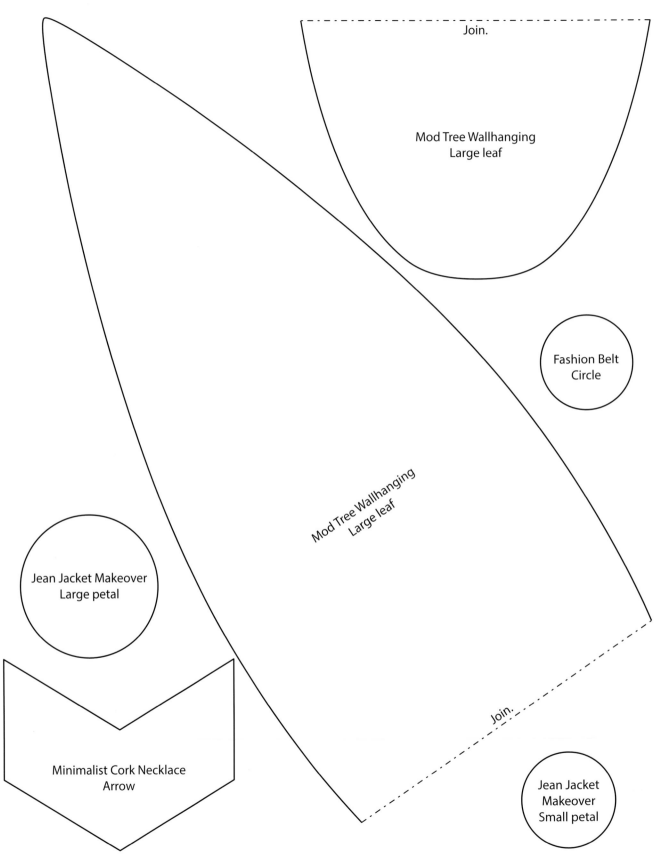

Join.

Mod Tree Wallhanging
Large leaf

Fashion Belt
Circle

Mod Tree Wallhanging
Large leaf

Jean Jacket Makeover
Large petal

Join.

Minimalist Cork Necklace
Arrow

Jean Jacket
Makeover
Small petal

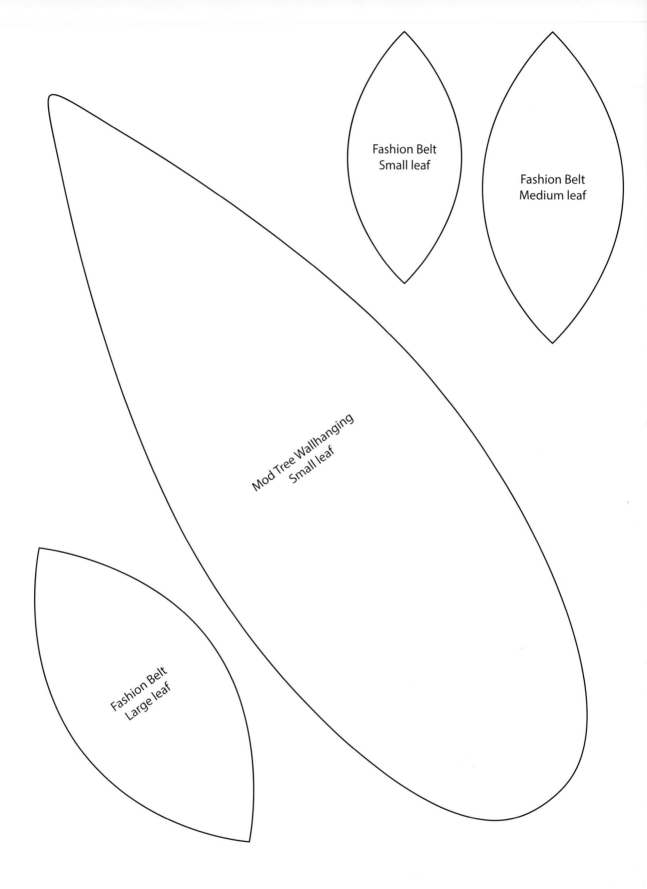

Fashion Belt
Small leaf

Fashion Belt
Medium leaf

Mod Tree Wallhanging
Small leaf

Fashion Belt
Large leaf

resources

The following is a list of terrific suppliers and brands that I use and trust. Don't be afraid to try out other suppliers, however—there are so many wonderful companies out there making great things. Remember to shop local when you can!

CORK FABRIC

Sallie Tomato
sallietomato.com

FABRIC

Art Gallery Fabrics
artgalleryfabrics.com

Cloud9 Fabrics
cloud9fabrics.com

Rifle Paper Co.
riflepaperco.com

NOTIONS AND HARDWARE

Sallie Tomato
sallietomato.com

Superior Threads
superiorthreads.com

**C&T Publishing
(Freezer Paper Sheets)**
ctpub.com

FUSIBLE INTERFACING

Bosal Fashion Fuse
bosalonline.com

Pellon Shape-Flex
pellonprojects.com

FUSIBLE FLEECE BATTING

Bosal Light Fusible Batting
bosalonline.com

Pellon Fusible Fleece
pellonprojects.com

FUSIBLE FOAM

Bosal In-R-Form double-sided fusible
bosalonline.com

Pellon Flex-Foam
pellonprojects.com

ByAnnie's Soft and Stable
byannie.com

MORE ABOUT CORK FABRIC

APCOR
apcor.pt/en

Portugalia Cork
portugaliacork.com/about-cork

about the author

Jessica Sallie Kapitanski has been creatively sewing and crafting since the age of five. She studied entrepreneurship at the University of Wisconsin-Whitewater and now operates and designs for her own business, Sallie Tomato. Jessica teaches classes locally, online, and across the country. She is especially addicted to sewing bags and writing patterns for them, which she sells in her online shop and through fabric shops worldwide. Her innovative designs and products aim to attract the next generation of sewing enthusiasts while appealing to current sewists. Her hope is that when others make one of her projects they will think, "Wow, I made this!" Jessica currently lives in Wisconsin with her family and adorable dachshund, Buddy.

VISIT JESSICA ONLINE AND FOLLOW ON SOCIAL MEDIA!

Website: sallietomato.com

Pinterest: /pinsallietomato

Facebook: /sallietomatopatterns

Instagram: @sallietomatopatterns

Want even more creative content?

Make it,
snap it,
share it
using
#ctpublishing